"*Queer Rites* is as magical and special as they come. The market is far from cornered on topics of queerness and magic, but the rites outlined here would be relevant and unique no matter what."

—**CASSANDRA SNOW**, author of *Queering Your Craft* and *Queering the Tarot*

"In an age wherein personal milestones have devolved into notch marks of capitalist accumulation, *Queer Rites* reclaims the sacredness of the stages of life unique to the queer experience of our modern world."

—**TOMÁS PROWER**, author of *Queer Magic*

"With a friendly, warm, and encouraging voice, *Queer Rites* is the wise friend a queer Witch needs to help them navigate the greatest moments of a magickal life. No matter how they identify, there are crucial things for a Witch to utilize within these pages."

—**COURTNEY WEBER**, author of *Sacred Tears*

"I came out as a witch and as a queer man in the 1970s and I can only imagine how much my life would have been enriched if *Queer Rites* had been available then."

—**IVO DOMINGUEZ JR.**, author of the Witch's Sun Sign series

"*Queer Rites* addresses the demand for rites of passage that speak directly to the experiences of LGBTQIAP2S+ people.... An invaluable resource, empowering queer magickal practitioners to embrace their true selves with confidence and spiritual depth."

—**MAT AURYN**, author of *Psychic Witch*

"Enfys has taken the elements of Queer life that for so many have gone unnoticed and uncelebrated and offered a cohesive, powerful, and magical way to ritualize them. This is a handbook for individuals, groups, and communities alike."

—**KRISTOFFER HUGHES**, author of *The Book of Druidry*

"An incredible and must-have resource of rituals for the queer practitioner.... and a necessary addition to any library for those seeking to understand and create more inclusive rites for their greater community as well."

—**LAURA TEMPEST ZAKROFF**, author of *Sigil Witchery* and *Anatomy of a Witch*

"A compassionate, encouraging guide to the ritual expression of queerness in all its forms. Enfys speaks to the reader as a wise and trusted friend and makes room for the doubts, anxieties, and (ultimately) joys that come from exploring queer identity."
—JACK CHANEK, author of *Queen of All Witcheries*

"Incorporating concepts from modern Pagan religions, queer history, mythology, Hermetic Qabala, and Tarot, Enfys has crafted a truly necessary and practical guide.... Enfys makes the working of these rites accessible to everyone, regardless of spiritual background."
—THUMPER FORGE, coauthor of *Virgo Witch*

"An incredible map through the evolving spiritual experience of queer people. This collection of rituals, ideas, and activities offers potent and profound ways to approach the different crossroads of life, from identity celebration to community involvement."
—IRENE GLASSE, author of *Blackfeather Mystery School*

"In this book, you will find rituals to honor, celebrate, and sit with the various milestone experiences unique to, or common within, the queer community. In these pages, you will find a friend to help you navigate your own fabulous path of self discovery."
—J. R. MASCARO, author of *Seal, Sigil & Call*

"Queer people have experiences that are so unique to our lives, we deserve to mark them with equally unique rites. From supporting challenging times to celebrating queer joy, *Queer Rites* will be known as an essential grimoire long into the future."
—DAVID SALISBURY, author of *Witchcraft Activism*

"An essential library component for those of us who've had little to no precedent up to now for our personal paths and passages as Queer-identified practitioners.... An inspiring, affirming, inclusive set of ideas."
—S. J. TUCKER, musician and witch

QUEER
RITES

QUEER RITES

A Magickal Grimoire to Honor Your Milestones with Pride

ENFYS J BOOK

WOODBURY, MINNESOTA

FIRST EDITION
First Printing, 2025

Book design by Christine Ha
Cover design by Shira Atakpu
Interior Illustrations
    Astrological, alchemical, and planetary symbols and figures 1–15 by the Llewellyn Art Department
    Figures 16–23 by Mara Benowitz

Llewellyn Publications is a registered trademark of Llewellyn Worldwide Ltd.

Library of Congress Cataloging-in-Publication Data (Pending)
ISBN: 978-0-7387-7610-1

Llewellyn Publications
A Division of Llewellyn Worldwide Ltd.
2143 Wooddale Drive
Woodbury, MN 55125-2989
www.llewellyn.com

Printed in the United States of America

OTHER BOOKS BY ENFYS J. BOOK

Queer Qabala
Sagittarius Witch (coauthor)

DISCLAIMER

Studying, working magick, and engaging in ritual can sometimes bring up challenging emotions and situations. If you should ever find yourself in serious mental or emotional distress after a magickal working or ritual, please seek professional psychological help. The magickal operations and invitations for practice in this book are not a replacement for professional medical attention, mental health care, or legal advice.

*To everyone who is
trying to be their most
authentic, fabulous self.*

CONTENTS

FOREWORD
Ariana Serpentine

People's lives are filled with milestones—shared points of progress that map with the experiences of others, things that draw us together and make us realize we have things in common with other people and that we are not alone. Coming-of-age ceremonies, whether religious or strictly cultural, are common enough, as are marriages and funerals. There are also different sorts of initiations, such as rituals where you join a particular group and become part of a new collective identity. There are the unofficial milestones, often not marked by ceremony: losing your first tooth, your first period, your first kiss, the first time you encounter death, and others.

Many of the milestones that are celebrated in modern Western society are ones that are complicated for queer people. You can be excited about your first kiss, but can you tell your parents about it without fear of being kicked out of your home or worse? Up until very recently in the United States, marriage for many queer couples was out of the question, and it still is in many places worldwide (not to mention constant efforts to undo the right to marriage equality by retrograde forces once it has been established). Going through some kind of rite of passage of "becoming a man/woman" when you are both, neither, or not the one that people perceive you as can be painful and damaging. Also, families often pay for and coordinate weddings and funerals; what happens when someone's family refuses to do so because of the person's sexuality or gender?

These moments of our lives, meant to be treasured and marked as progress, are marred by culture that dehumanizes us. There are so many things that queer people are not able to participate in because of that dehumanization, and many of those are things that are taken for granted by the majority of people as being a regular and expected part of life. You go to kindergarten, get into high school, have your first kiss, are taken out drinking when you come to legal age, maybe go to the university or maybe get married and be a parent and work, raise your children until they leave your home and then prepare to care for your grandchildren, guide your grandchildren until it's time for you to die, after which everyone who knew you gathers and speaks good words about your life. So many of those things are denied to queer people or made difficult or painful by discrimination and bigotry.

If we do celebrate, we often celebrate in private. Maybe we celebrate alone, or maybe with the other queer people we've found. We can celebrate with the others like us who don't turn us away and who love and honor us rather than hate or merely tolerate us. We've developed some of our own rites of passage, but because our lives come from so many different places and because of the diversity of queer experiences, no one set of milestones or ceremonies is going to work for everyone or even most people. We need to get creative.

I did a series of ceremonies over the course of a week when I was ready to come out as trans. I sacralized my first estrogen dose and have been doing the same ever since. I went out for the first time dressed in all women's clothing to a queer Valentine's Day ball. I called on my ancestors of blood in a ritual and introduced myself to them as a woman and gave them my new name. I did my best in my own life, on my own, to mark these moments that I found important. I believe that a lot of us do in our own ways. It would have been nice to have guidelines or suggestions to help me work through these moments of transition. It would have been great to have community to do these things with, most of which I did alone.

That is why this book is so important. It is to me, personally, as I read through it and saw suggestions for things that I, as a queer and trans witch and Pagan, would have liked to have done earlier in my life. Many of the rituals are things that I could still do or adapt to do years after the thing has been done to give a sense of finality or closure. I personally intend to adapt and perform some of these rites myself because I think that they would help to tie up loose ends that time has left untied. I wish I had this book when I was a silly queer hippie going to flamboyant, clothing-optional Pagan festivals in my late teens and early twenties; I think it would have helped me progress in a healthier way, and I think the variety of rituals and suggestions would have made me consider options I didn't realize that I had.

That's one of the other wonderful things about *Queer Rites*: while it has many ceremonies and ideas for rites that you may already want to perform, there are also suggestions for things that you may not have thought of. That opening of opportunity and understanding is much of what is driving the queer revolution that we are seeing these days. Many people didn't realize that there were words for things that they've held inside their whole lives, and learning that there are, and that others share similar experiences, can be a huge revelation. Some people had never considered the possibility that they could love a gender they weren't raised to, or be a gender that others didn't perceive in them. Every person who comes out and brings their radiant individuality into view is providing an example to someone else who has never seen or heard of someone else like them, someone who felt the way that they do or is doing the things that they want to do. I think that's powerful and awe-inspiring to witness, and is part of the blossoming and unfolding of the Divine in human nature and the world.

Queer Rites provides individual rituals as well as useful suggestions on correspondences that are helpful for coordinating the spiritual work. It also provides options and suggestions and ideas for rites that readers may never have considered in the first place. It gives both solid structure and abundant choices to craft rituals to help mark those important milestones both alone and with community.

I long for a world where queer folks don't face the challenges that we do today. I dream of a time when our kids or their kids won't have to make a big deal about coming out, or perhaps will make a big deal about coming out and not meet with any resistance or pushback. I want a world where we can be tolerated, but also one where we can and will be celebrated, and I think that any work in that direction is a benefit to us all. Enfys's book is a stride forward in realizing that dream. Through this book and books like this, we can earnestly have these conversations about not just our right to exist but how we wish to exist and what we want to be.

Patheos blogger Arhiana Platten wrote: "Rites and rituals open hearts and clear minds. They help us to embody reverence and allow us to get in touch with our emotions and desires. They provide safe ways to make a change."[1] So keep your mind open to the options and opportunities that present themselves in this work, and you'll find it easy to adapt them to your own needs and life. Enfys can

---

1. Arhiana Platten, *Rites and Rituals: Harnessing the Power of Sacred Ceremony* (Bethesda, MD: Brave Healer Productions, 2023), 7.

be your guide through considering these vital celebrations and moments in your life. I believe that in years to come, *Queer Rites* will help many of us liminal people navigate our most personal and powerful moments, the times that we stand at the thresholds of what was, what is, and what can be, and in doing so open the way to new futures for ourselves and the generations of queer descendants to come.

INTRODUCTION

In 2020, I decided it was time to change my name.

I'm nonbinary, and at that point, I had lived with a very traditionally feminine name for forty-one years. My name felt like a shackle weighing down my attempts to express myself and my gender in an authentic way.

If you've never gone through a name change before, you may not be aware of how long and complicated a process it is. It is so complicated—even in the trans-friendly state of Maryland—that someone like me, who is a professional project manager adept at wrangling lots of little details and moving parts, was completely overwhelmed by the sheer number of steps and contingencies involved.

Each of these steps felt like its own sort of ritual: they all needed preparation and materials, and each had concrete outcomes. The steps I went through impacted me on a physical level and, to some degree, an emotional level, but no one step constituted the actual change of the name within *myself*. None of the bureaucratic steps impacted me spiritually or told my soul and my deities that *this* was my new name. In other words, something was missing in the process.

I knew I needed a magickal ritual to release my old name and integrate my new name into myself, but I had no idea how to start constructing such a thing, even though I'd been writing rituals for spiritual groups for several years at that point.

I asked one of the elders of my tradition, Robin Fennelly, for help. And she went above and beyond, crafting a highly personal ritual with timing based on my own natal chart, and even creating a sigil from the new name. I made some adaptations and additions to make it resonate even more deeply with the focus of my spiritual work at the time, and conducted the ritual the day after my birthday, when there was a full moon and a lunar eclipse as well as some helpful transits from my natal chart. Doing it after my birthday also gave the ritual the energy of both honoring the anniversary of the day I was born and pulling away from the name my parents gifted to me shortly after my birth.

The experience was deeply impactful for me, and in the course of it, I realized how critical and yet how neglected rites of passage are in our dominant overculture. When they are acknowledged, rites of passage are often heavily commercialized (weddings), made light of (milestone birthdays), or incredibly dry and intended for such broad audiences that they lose personal meaning (graduation ceremonies). Where and why have we lost our way with rites of passage?

I can't help but think that our disconnection from rites of passage and our lack of creating meaningful, personal rituals around them may contribute to entire generations of people feeling lost. Marking key moments of growth and change gives us an anchor for the self: something to hold onto, something to acknowledge how far we've come and where we're going, and an opportunity for us to evolve even further, with magickal assistance. As queer people in particular, our lives and milestones differ from the mainstream, so there's even less of a script for how to handle them than those in the mainstream have to work with. We can feel adrift and disconnected even more so than others do, especially if we are disconnected from our families of origin.

WHAT'S A QUEER RITE OF PASSAGE?

Queer people go through all kinds of unique milestones and rites of passage as we grow into our true selves. Whether it's coming out, taking your first dose of hormones, experiencing a polyamorous handfasting, or acknowledging chosen family, we have much to celebrate. We also have much to grieve. Sometimes it's vital for our mental and physical health to cut ties from family and friends who are unsupportive of our authentic selves, for example. There are also more intimate milestone moments when we discover new things about our own identities. We have myriad opportunities to enter into these rites of passage thoughtfully and spiritually, to open ourselves to guidance as we navigate the sometimes-treacherous waters of being queer humans.

A rite of passage can happen regardless of whether there is a formalized ritual attached to it. But by adding a magickal ritual component, you can connect your experiences more deeply to your spiritual life, invite in your spirit and deity guides to experience the rite with you and provide guidance, and commemorate the occasion in a deeply meaningful way that encourages contemplation and growth. Whether by yourself, with trusted friends, or spiritual community, you can acknowledge your rites of passage and make them resonate more deeply within you by building rituals around them.

In determining which rituals to include in this book, I decided I wanted to focus, as much as possible, on rites of passage unique to the queer experience as opposed to rituals for general life experiences adapted to a queer perspective (e.g., a queer graduation ritual) or rituals that could apply to a wide array of people inside or outside the queer community (e.g., a ritual for healing after a breakup). A queer rite of passage is an evolutionary experience mostly, if not exclusively, experienced by LGBTQIAP2S+ (lesbian, gay, bisexual, transgender, queer, intersex, asexual/aromantic/agender, pansexual, Two-Spirit, and beyond) people. There are some rites of passage included that are shared between queer people and other marginalized groups, and some that can be easily adapted for a broader audience, but for the most part, these are things queer people go through related to our queerness.

WHO IS THIS BOOK FOR?

If you are an LGBTQIAP2S+ (henceforward referred to as *queer* because the acronym changes with some regularity and *queer* is more all-encompassing) magickal practitioner of any age and have gone through or are about to go through a rite of passage you feel needs a magickal component, or if you are interested in rituals that can help you grow as a person and find your inner truth, this book is for you.

Here are a few signs that you may need a magickal rite of passage in your life:

+ Feeling stuck in the middle of a life transition
+ Wanting to grow and deepen your understanding of yourself
+ A general feeling that something is wrong or incomplete
+ Wanting to more tightly weave your queer identity into your magickal practice

One of the themes and terms you'll see a lot in this book is *sovereignty*. The concept of sovereignty is a very important one in life, boundaries, and magickal practice. *Sovereignty* means *you belong to you.* Only you get to determine your identity. As queer people, our identities are often called into question, denied, or belittled, so embracing your personal power and your self-ownership is critical to your self-worth, mental health, and peace with yourself in the face of the naysayers. The rituals in this book aim to remind you of your personal sovereignty and help you embrace it.

I'm so excited to share these rituals with you. I hope you will find them useful, profound, and meaningful. I hope they will bring positive change into your life and make you more confident in sharing your unique and wonderful self with the world.

PART 1: WHAT GOES INTO a RITUAL?

Chapter 1
RITUAL BASICS

A *ritual*, in a magickal context, is an event that includes creating a magickal container (also known as sacred space) and doing a magickal action within that container, with specific steps preceding and following, all in service to a specific goal. It is a meaningful experience that can shift our perception and create change in our reality. "Rituals speak to us in ways that words aren't capable of," writes witch and author Phoenix LeFae in her book *A Witch's Guide to Creating & Performing Rituals That Actually Work*.[2]

A ritual is more than a spell: it's an *event*. Even if it's just for one person! A spell may be a component of a ritual, but the structure of a ritual is more complex than casting a spell.

WHAT IS THE PURPOSE OF A RITUAL?

Rituals have a number of different purposes. Some of the rituals in this book are meant to give you time and space to explore something hidden deep within you or work toward healing. Some are celebrations of finding your inner truth or celebrations of relationships, both platonic and romantic. Others help you define, process, integrate, and celebrate a moment when something in you has changed, or they may push something within yourself *to* change. Some are intended to help you build confidence to face challenging things. Some are designed to help you release things that are no longer conducive to your growth. What they all share in common is the

---

2. Phoenix LeFae, *A Witch's Guide to Creating & Performing Rituals That Actually Work* (Woodbury, MN: Llewellyn Worldwide, 2023), 2.

intent to have a long-term positive impact on your soul, your life, and your evolution as a person—even the rituals that may be emotionally painful to experience.

WHO CAN PERFORM THESE RITUALS?

Anyone can lead the rituals in this book, even people who are new to magickal work. These rituals are written to be easy to follow and perform for magickal practitioners of all skill levels. While some magickal groups and traditions may restrict group ritual leadership to people of a certain level of experience, you can perform your own rituals for yourself anytime. Most of the rituals in this book are intended to be done by yourself.

THE FORMAT OF A RITUAL

Rituals do not require grand theatricality to be effective, and many people do not have the time, ability, or resources to create elaborate rituals. Most of the rituals in this book are very simple, require only a handful of inexpensive or free supplies, and can be completed in twenty to sixty minutes. This is by design. I wanted to make sure this book was as inclusive as possible to a wide variety of magickal traditions and practices, people with financial constraints, people with limited space for performing rituals, people without a ton of time to themselves to devote to their magickal practice, and so on. A book of elaborate rituals requiring lots of fancy and hard-to-find ingredients may feel *witchier* but would be inaccessible to people with modest means or less experience with witchcraft. The rituals in this book are designed to be simple but effective.

That said, you can take these rituals as a starting point to create something more elaborate if you like! By starting with something simple, I've left room for you to customize the ritual and make it your own in a way that makes sense for you and your unique practice. You can add any kind of regular ritual components you use in your personal practice, any personal artifacts or magickal tools you'd like to include, and anything that makes you feel more deeply in ritual headspace, like wearing specific ritual garb, lighting incense, or playing specific ritual music.

One of the tricky things about writing this book is that some people will be approaching it with a very defined and established magickal practice and way of doing things, whereas others might be very new to witchcraft and ritual. While the parts of each ritual in this book are designed to accomplish a specific tried-and-true function to make rituals more effective, if you see anything in the ritual template that does not work for you or your practice, replace it with something that works better for you, as long as your substitute practice does the same thing that part of the ritual was intended to do. It's also okay to improvise in the moment if you feel drawn to do something differently or add something to the ritual. Trust your instincts and the spirits guiding you.

Most of these rituals are best done solo, in part because they are meant to be intensely personal and give you space for exploration without being self-conscious. A few really only work in a group context, because they are meant to be experiences of group affirmation and celebration. And some can be adapted either way. In those cases, I've noted suggestions at the end of the ritual for how you can adapt it.

Make sure you read each ritual carefully, ideally a few times, before you commit to doing it. You'll be more comfortable and confident working through the ritual if you have a sense of what to expect.

You may choose to adapt one or more of these rituals to perform on behalf of someone else. In that case, it's important to work with that person ahead of time to understand what would make the ritual most meaningful for them, what kinds of things they want and don't want included. Then you can customize the ritual to fit their needs. Sometimes, the ritual template I offer won't work for the situation you have in mind, and you will need to write a whole new ritual from scratch. That can be daunting, especially if you haven't written a ritual before, but I'm hopeful that the content in the first two chapters of this book will give you enough ideas of what to do that you can confidently tackle this challenge. For a deeper introduction to ritual writing, I recommend the book *A Witch's Guide to Creating & Performing Rituals That Actually Work* by Phoenix LeFae.

Each ritual in this book has standardized sections at the beginning to help you determine which partners and energies you want to work with in the ritual, recommended timing, materials needed, and sensory and emotional energies to tie in. It's important to consider these things ahead of time and make choices for how to approach your ritual that best fit you, your practice, and the goals of your specific rite of passage. Let's dive into each of these parts of ritual planning in more detail.

PARTNERS AND ENERGIES

Almost every ritual includes a section that lists potential partners and energies that may be helpful in the ritual. These include deities and ancestors as well as planetary, elemental, Qabala, and tarot correspondences. Adding these energetic powers can enhance your work. But do you *have* to use them?

No. In fact, I would encourage you to only use partners and energies that resonate with your practice and ones you've already built a relationship with. Pick one or two from the list that you work with already, or swap in partners and energies that weren't suggested if they are part of your practice and you think they would be a good fit.

Since work with deities in particular can be highly subjective, you may disagree with my choices for these rituals, or you may have a preferred pantheon that's not included. I encourage you to use whatever deities, spirits, and energetic forms you feel are most appropriate for each ritual. And if you prefer not to work with any partners or energies, that's fine. They can boost the power of the ritual, but they are not required.

DEITIES

You may notice some deities are used repeatedly throughout this book. That's because there are certain deities who are particularly aligned with queer experiences. A number of deities are notably shapeshifters and genderfluid (e.g., Loki, Odinn, and Dionysus) or both-and-neither binary genders (e.g., Hapi, Asushunamir, and Atum), and they are all ideal to work with for any rituals related to gender exploration and affirmation.[3] Many are known for helping people claim their personal power (e.g., Freyja, the Morrigan, and Rhiannon[4]) and freedom to be their true selves (e.g., Loki, Dionysus, and Ma'at). Some are particularly resonant for and popular among transgender polytheists (e.g., Kybele, Freyja, Freyr, and Loki), and some are particularly resonant for nonheterosexual polytheists

---

3. Storm Faerywolf, *The Satyr's Kiss: Queer Men, Sex Magic & Modern Witchcraft* (Woodbury, MN: Llewellyn Worldwide, 2022), 68–70; "Hapi: Egyptian God of the Inundation," Britannica, accessed May 14, 2024, https://www.britannica.com/topic/Hapi.
4. Mhara Starling, *Welsh Witchcraft: A Guide to the Spirits, Lore, and Magic of Wales* (Woodbury, MN: Llewellyn Publications, 2022), 89.

(e.g., Apollo, Artemis, Athena, Pan, Eros, Dionysus, Hermes, Set, and Horus).[5] If you do not currently work with specific deities that affirm your queerness, your magickal practice and self-understanding may be improved by working with one or more of these deities as part of your spiritual journey.

ANCESTORS

Many of these rituals include the recommendation or opportunity to work with queer ancestors. Even if you have not been historically comfortable including ancestors as part of your magickal work, perhaps due to feelings of disconnection or discomfort with your family of origin, I encourage you to consider adding some form of queer ancestor veneration to your practice.

When I mention queer ancestors, I don't just mean queer people you are related to or descended from—though we all have queer ancestors by blood or other familial relation and may or may not know their names or histories. The concept of *ancestors* transcends those we are related to and also includes ancestors of affinity and choice: meaning that people throughout history with whom we have things in common, or with whom we choose to associate, are also our ancestors. Our queerness connects us to all the queer people throughout history. If you're uncomfortable using the word *ancestor* to describe these beings' relationship with you, you may substitute *forerunners* or *the mighty dead*.

Much like working with queer deities, working with queer ancestors can benefit your magickal practice and sense of self. There's a lot we can learn from previously incarnated queer humans. You can connect to the general stream of power of all queer ancestors, or you can work with specific queer ancestors. Here are some you might consider working with:

---

5. Ariana Serpentine, *Sacred Gender: Create Trans & Nonbinary Spiritual Connections* (Woodbury, MN: Llewellyn Publications, 2022), 72–80; Misha Magdalene, *Outside the Charmed Circle: Exploring Gender & Sexuality in Magical Practice* (Woodbury, MN: Llewellyn Publications, 2020), 128–137; Cassandra Snow, *Queering Your Craft: Witchcraft from the Margins* (Newburyport, MA: Weiser Books, 2020), 115–116; Faerywolf, *The Satyr's Kiss*, 68, 71, 72, 74, 76, 77–78.

Audre Lorde (1934–1992)

Black lesbian feminist, writer, poet, professor, activist, and philosopher who pointed out the failings of the civil rights movement to address women's issues and the feminist movement's failure to address non-white women's issues.[6]

Frank Kameny (1925–2011)

Gay activist instrumental in removing homosexuality from the American Psychiatric Association's *Diagnostic and Statistical Manual of Mental Disorders* and in ensuring queer people can hold security clearances in the federal government of the United States.[7]

Harvey Milk (1930–1978)

Gay activist and the first openly gay man elected to public office in California.[8]

Marsha P. Johnson (1945–1992)

Black transgender queer rights activist and sex worker who participated in the Stonewall uprising and cofounded, with Sylvia Rivera, an organization to help homeless queer youth.[9]

Sylvia Rivera (1951–2002)

Latina transgender queer rights activist and sex worker who participated in the Stonewall uprising and cofounded, with Marsha P. Johnson, an organization to help homeless queer youth.[10]

6. Meg-John Barker and Jules Scheele, *Queer: A Graphic History* (London: Icon Books, 2016), 43.
7. David W. Dunlap, "Franklin Kameny, Gay Rights Pioneer, Dies at 86," *New York Times*, October 12, 2011, https://www.nytimes.com/2011/10/13/us/franklin-kameny-gay-rights-pioneer-dies-at-86.html.
8. Lenny Giteck, "Harvey Milk's Original *Advocate* Obituary from 1979," *Advocate*, November 27, 2018, https://www.advocate.com/politics/2018/11/27/harvey-milks-original-advocate-obituary-1979.
9. Emma Rothberg, "Marsha P. Johnson" National Women's History Museum, accessed May 14, 2024, https://www.womenshistory.org/education-resources/biographies/marsha-p-johnson.
10. Emma Rothberg, "Sylvia Rivera," National Women's History Museum, accessed February 23, 2024, https://www.womenshistory.org/education-resources/biographies/sylvia-rivera.

PLANETS AND ELEMENTS

I've included planets and elements you can work with in your rituals. These can be used to inspire your altar decorations, as each planet and element corresponds to specific colors and sigils you can incorporate. If you regularly work with the spirits of the planets or elements, you can also call to them when you invite in spirits in the ritual. Adding symbolic representations of or invitations to aligned planets and elements can provide additional layers of power and focus to your ritual.

Planetary Color and Symbol Correspondences

Celestial Body	Color	Symbol
Sun	Yellow or gold	☉
Moon	Purple	☾
Mercury	Orange	☿
Venus	Green	♀
Mars	Red	♂
Jupiter	Blue	♃
Saturn	Black	♄
Uranus	Gray	♅
Neptune	White	♆

Elemental Symbols

These color correspondences and symbols are not universally used but are very common among Pagan and polytheist groups.

Element	Color	Alchemical symbol	Altar decoration ideas
Earth	Green	▽	Soil, salt, rocks, plants, flowers, heavy and dark-colored crystals, images or figures of land-based animals
Air	Yellow	△	Feathers, lightweight and light-colored crystals, clear glass, images or figures of birds or winged insects
Fire	Red	△	Incense, candles, red crystals, chili and other hot spices, images or figures of dragons or salamanders
Water	Blue	▽	Cups, bowls, or chalices, dishes of water, blue crystals, images or figures of water-dwelling creatures like fish

TAROT AND QABALA

The Partners and Energies section includes tarot and Qabala correspondences. Tarot is a divination tool that consists of seventy-eight cards divided into a major arcana and a minor arcana. The major arcana features twenty-two cards of big concepts or milestones in growth. The minor arcana features fifty-six cards, typically about day-to-day life things, arranged in four suits: wands, cups, pentacles or coins, and swords.

Each card has specific imagery associated with it. Hermetic Qabala, meanwhile, is an occult framework with origins in Jewish mysticism, used to understand and experience life and the universe.[11] It is a tool for elevating one's consciousness, for deepening one's understanding of oneself, and for discovering and embracing the whole of manifested and unmanifested reality through the Tree of Life glyph.

Hermetic Qabala is a practice that was developed over hundreds of years, often in collaboration with Jewish scholars, and is available to all occult practitioners, whereas the Jewish devotional practice of Kabbalah is understood to be a closed practice limited to only Jewish practitioners.[12] The two practices share some overlap, including the Tree of Life glyph and Hebrew names of the spheres, but are fundamentally different approaches to the same spiritual tool. If you use Hermetic Qabala in your practice, it is important to use it respectfully, taking care to understand and acknowledge its origins.

I include these two magickal systems and symbol sets as options for powers to engage with in your rituals, because magick works best when you have multiple layers of symbolism resonating with the energy you are trying to work with. Both Qabala and tarot are well-established and have rich and varied sets of symbolic correspondences associated with them. If you are familiar with either of these systems, you can incorporate them into your altar decorations, meditate upon them before or during the ritual, or invoke them as partners and energies you call into your ritual to add some extra juice to your working.

For example, if a ritual lists Hod, one of the spheres on the Tree of Life, as a possible power to align with, you could include an orange-colored crystal, an orange altar cloth, an eight-sided polyhedron, or other symbols aligned with Hod as part of your altar setup, and you may choose to spend part of your time before or during ritual meditating upon and connecting with that sphere. You may also call to the spirit of Hod when you are calling in partners to join you in the ritual.

As another example, if a ritual says the Lovers card could be a possible power to work with, pull the Lovers card from your tarot deck and place it on the altar. Spend some time gazing at it and meditating upon it, either before or during the ritual, to tap into the flavor of energy you are trying to work with. What does

11. Enfys J. Book, *Queer Qabala* (Woodbury, MN: Llewellyn Publications, 2022), 15–23.
12. Christopher Penczak, *The Temple of High Witchcraft: Ceremonies, Spheres, and the Witches' Qabalah* (Woodbury, MN: Llewellyn Publications, 2017), 84; Israel Regardie, *A Garden of Pomegranates: An Outline of the Qabalah* (Los Angeles, CA: New Falcon, 2019), xxii.

this card mean to you? Can you put yourself inside the scene within the card to understand it more deeply? What kinds of thought processes does it trigger in your brain? How do you feel physically and energetically when you focus your gaze on the card?

If you're just getting started with Qabala, here are the number, planetary, and color correspondences for each sphere to inspire your altar setup.

QABALA CORRESPONDENCES

Sphere	Number	Celestial body	Color
Kether	1	Neptune	White
Chokmah	2	Uranus	Gray
Binah	3	Saturn	Black
Chesed	4	Jupiter	Royal blue
Geburah	5	Mars	Red
Tiphareth	6	Sun	Gold
Netzach	7	Venus	Forest green
Hod	8	Mercury	Orange
Yesod	9	Moon	Purple
Malkuth	10	Earth	Citrine, olive, russet, and black

If you are not comfortable with Qabala or tarot, simply do not use these correspondences. You may have other symbol sets you find more useful that you can include, such as animals, plants, crystals, talismans, numerology, and sacred geometry. Adding additional layers of symbolism related to the working you are doing will enhance the power of the working, particularly if that symbol set is close to your heart and is a part of your existing magickal practice.

The Bottom Line

If you are a seasoned practitioner with a specific set of deities, spirits, and correspondences that are particularly resonant for you in your magickal practice, please use them in these rituals. If you do not have a set of spirits or correspondences you regularly work with, the rituals in this book will be more powerful if you first spend some time researching, learning about, and building a relationship with some of the ones I suggest. The books in the recommended reading section can get you started learning more about these deities and systems, and your queer magickal practice can benefit greatly from doing so.

Recommended Timing

You can add even more power to your ritual by conducting it during times that are more favorable to the energy you're trying to work with and the outcomes you're trying to achieve. Though I don't believe the movements of the planets are the *cause* of any human events here on earth, I do believe the universe is basically a giant fractal, and things on the macro level tend to reflect things on the micro level. To that end, there are times when the vibe of the universe better fits the type of magickal work you're trying to do, and the more you try to align your work to those times, the easier and more effective that work will be.

Astrologers have a powerful tool set they can call upon to determine ideal timing for a ritual: when the planets are in specific signs, aspects, and transits. If you're an avid astrologer, I encourage you to use your skills to find some ideal times for your rite of passage rituals based on your natal chart, transits, and planetary aspects.

For those of us who aren't avid astrologers, to make things simpler and contribute to ease of planning, in this book I've suggested ritual timings based on planetary days of the week, planetary hours, and moon phases, rather than diving deep into planetary aspects and transits. I did this because some astrological events don't come around very often, and I don't want anyone to feel like they have to wait weeks, months, or years to do a rite of passage ritual.

If you want to dive deeper into the subject of astrology and magickal timing, I recommend Theresa Reed's *Astrology for Real Life* as a great introductory book on astrology. For a more advanced book on how you can use astrology in magick, I recommend *Practical Astrology for Witches and Pagans* by Ivo Dominguez Jr.

PLANETARY DAYS

For each ritual, I've suggested the most effective days of the week for the ritual to take place. The Sun, Moon, and first five planets in our solar system are assigned to days of the week. Each of these celestial bodies relates to certain areas of life and types of energy, which are useful to consider when planning your ritual. For example, by timing a ritual related to love on Venus day (Friday), or better yet, during Venus hour on Venus Day, you're paddling with the current of the universe, increasing the working's effectiveness and helping the magick flow more easily. The planets assigned to each day of the week are:

Sunday: Sun

The energy of the Sun is best for rituals related to healing, celebration, hope, success, the self, and finding clarity in a situation.

Monday: Moon

The energy of the Moon is best for rituals related to emotions, intuition, finding what is hidden, glamours, and psychism.

Tuesday: Mars

The energy of Mars is best for rituals related to sex, energy, justice, protection, and conflict.

Wednesday: Mercury

The energy of Mercury is best for rituals related to communication, intellect, travel, money, and education.

Thursday: Jupiter

The energy of Jupiter is best for rituals related to luck, talent, risks, abundance, and leadership.

Friday: Venus

The energy of Venus is best for rituals related to love, pleasure, and relationships of all kinds.

Saturday: Saturn

The energy of Saturn is best for rituals related to challenges, endings, limitations, business, boundaries, and discipline.

PLANETARY HOURS

In addition to planetary days, we have planetary hours. Planetary hours change every day. They are determined by taking the total number of minutes from sunrise to sunset and dividing it by twelve, then doing the same with the number of minutes from sunset to sunrise, and assigning each of those twenty-four chunks of time to the planets in a specific order that changes each day of the week. Each planet has a few hours a day assigned to it. *Planetary hour* is a bit of a misnomer because they are not exactly an hour—the duration varies because the time from sunrise to sunset and sunset to sunrise varies. The easiest way to determine when a specific planet's hours are on a specific day is by searching online for "planetary hours calculator" or by consulting a planetary hours app. When you can't conduct your ritual on the ideal planetary day of the week, you can try to align it to that planet's hour on a different day. Or you can increase a ritual's impact by planning it for the same planetary hour and day of the week, or add a dynamic element by representing two different planets' energies by choosing the planetary hour of one and planetary day of another.

If you want to do the planetary hours math yourself without using an app, here is the process.

Calculating Planetary Hours

Find the sunrise and sunset times for the day you want to perform your ritual. Calculate the minutes between sunrise and sunset, then between sunset and the following day's sunrise. Divide each total number of minutes by twelve. That is the length of each daytime and nighttime planetary hour for that day.

Starting at sunrise, add the number of minutes for the daytime planetary hour to get the time to start hour two, then add that same number of minutes again to get the start of hour three, and so on. Do the same thing for night using the number of minutes for the nighttime planetary hour and starting at sunset.

Consult the tables below to determine the ruler of each day's and night's planetary hour.

Each day starts with the ruling planet of that day. The order of the planetary hours follows the order of the spheres on the Tree of Life.

Planetary Hour Rulers—Daytime[13]

Hour	Sunday	Monday	Tuesday	Wednesday	Thursday	Friday	Saturday
1 (Starts at sunrise)	Sun	Moon	Mars	Mercury	Jupiter	Venus	Saturn
2	Venus	Saturn	Sun	Moon	Mars	Mercury	Jupiter
3	Mercury	Jupiter	Venus	Saturn	Sun	Moon	Mars
4	Moon	Mars	Mercury	Jupiter	Venus	Saturn	Sun
5	Saturn	Sun	Moon	Mars	Mercury	Jupiter	Venus
6	Jupiter	Venus	Saturn	Sun	Moon	Mars	Mercury
7	Mars	Mercury	Jupiter	Venus	Saturn	Sun	Moon
8	Sun	Moon	Mars	Mercury	Jupiter	Venus	Saturn
9	Venus	Saturn	Sun	Moon	Mars	Mercury	Jupiter
10	Mercury	Jupiter	Venus	Saturn	Sun	Moon	Mars
11	Moon	Mars	Mercury	Jupiter	Venus	Saturn	Sun
12 (ends at sunset)	Saturn	Sun	Moon	Mars	Mercury	Jupiter	Venus

13. Henry Cornelius Agrippa, *Three Books of Occult Philosophy*, trans. James Freake, ed. Donald Tyson (St. Paul, MN: Llewellyn Publications, 1993), 372.

Planetary Hour Rulers—Nighttime[14]

Hour	Sunday	Monday	Tuesday	Wednesday	Thursday	Friday	Saturday
1 (Starts at sunset)	Jupiter	Venus	Saturn	Sun	Moon	Mars	Mercury
2	Mars	Mercury	Jupiter	Venus	Saturn	Sun	Moon
3	Sun	Moon	Mars	Mercury	Jupiter	Venus	Saturn
4	Venus	Saturn	Sun	Moon	Mars	Mercury	Jupiter
5	Mercury	Jupiter	Venus	Saturn	Sun	Moon	Mars
6	Moon	Mars	Mercury	Jupiter	Venus	Saturn	Sun
7	Saturn	Sun	Moon	Mars	Mercury	Jupiter	Venus
8	Jupiter	Venus	Saturn	Sun	Moon	Mars	Mercury
9	Mars	Mercury	Jupiter	Venus	Saturn	Sun	Moon
10	Sun	Moon	Mars	Mercury	Jupiter	Venus	Saturn
11	Venus	Saturn	Sun	Moon	Mars	Mercury	Jupiter
12 (ends at sunrise)	Mercury	Jupiter	Venus	Saturn	Sun	Moon	Mars

14. Agrippa, *Three Books of Occult Philosophy*, 372.

Moon Phases

I've also suggested optimal moon phases—waxing, waning, full, or dark—for timing the rituals in this book. *Waxing* means that the illuminated part of the moon is growing, and *waning* means that the illuminated part of the moon is shrinking. For full and dark moon workings, ideally you'll want to do your work in the thirteen hours prior to when it's at its fullest or darkest, before the moon begins to enter its next phase. You can find moon phases and times by searching online or downloading an app. Many wall calendars and planners also note the moon phases.

Waxing Moon

The waxing moon is best for increasing something in your life or adding something new to your life (particularly new habits) and focusing on the outward presentation of things. It's great for creativity and inspiration.

Full Moon

Full moons are best for celebrating the culmination of something, manifesting something new after prior work to bring it into being, or creating stability in something.

Waning Moon

The waning moon is best for work to decrease or transform something in your life, or to do inner work. It's a great time for banishing and clearing magick.

Dark Moon

The dark moon is best for work to reveal things that are hidden and for removing something from your life.

Practical Concerns

Ultimately, the recommended timing for each ritual is simply that: recommended. If you can't time your ritual to match any of the suggestions in this book, that doesn't mean you shouldn't do the ritual. Issues of practicality are more important than timing your ritual perfectly with the astrological calendar: Make sure people are able to attend if it's a group ritual, ensure childcare is set up and you have space and time where you will be undisturbed for the length of the ritual, etc. Practical Paganism means sometimes our rituals aren't all timed perfectly, but the important thing is that we can still get great benefits from doing them.

RITUAL MATERIALS

The rituals in this book require a minimal amount of stuff to accomplish, and all the recommended materials are easy to obtain and either cheap or free. You are welcome to consider and include alternatives and additional materials you feel will add to the rite. For example, you may wish to place personal items or additional spiritual tools on the altar. If you can't find, can't afford, or can't find time to acquire or create the materials listed, I encourage you to look for alternatives you may already have on hand.

You may find yourself performing your ritual in a space where open flames are not allowed: for example, a dormitory room at a university. In this case, replace incense with a cotton ball sprayed or dabbed with a bit of essential oil or fragrance that is suitable for the working, and use battery-operated candles. For rituals where the candles must be burned down fully, instead leave the battery-operated candle on until its battery dies, then dispose of the dead batteries in an ecologically safe manner. For rituals where you are supposed to carve something onto a candle, use a Sharpie or paint pen to write it on the battery-operated candle instead. For rituals that ask you to burn a piece of paper, instead tear or cut it into tiny pieces.

Note that most rituals require a table or altar, which is not specifically listed in the ritual materials. You don't need to use anything fancy if you don't have a dedicated altar space. A TV tray with a cloth draped over it works perfectly well, and is, in fact, what my coven uses for elemental altars at our rituals. The corner of your dresser or other existing piece of furniture works fine as well. Even an overturned, sturdy cardboard box with a cloth draped over it will suffice; just don't burn anything on top of it, as it is less stable than a table.

Some rituals have the option to include traditional ritual tools, such as an athame (ritual blade) or wand. These tools are entirely optional. You can always use the index finger on your dominant hand in their place. Athames and wands are used to cast circles and direct energy into a specific point, which your fingers can also do perfectly well. If you do not have an athame or wand, don't sweat it. The casting will not suffer if you don't use one.

Some rituals invite you to include a comfort object, like a soft blanket, sweater, or stuffed animal if you so choose. A rite of passage is not an easy thing to experience, and exploring your deepest, innermost self can be emotionally fraught. Having something comforting with you can help ground you after an intense experience and remind you that you are safe. Feel free to include a comfort object in any ritual where you feel it would be beneficial to do so, even if it's not in the list of materials.

SENSORY AND EMOTIONAL ENERGIES

The parts of ritual that engage our senses and our emotions make a ritual feel *real*. Sensory elements in a ritual include visuals, textures, smells, sounds, and tastes. Engaging our senses in specific ways can be quite powerful because it snaps our attention to focus and tells our brain that we are doing something different and new. We are not simply reciting words in front of a table. We are doing *magick* in front of an *altar*, and we know that because we can smell incense, see the candle flame flicker, and hear a drumbeat played over our phone speaker or headphones. Appealing to your senses in specific ways can also be used to evoke specific emotions in rituals.

Emotions are helpful fuel for a ritual and can guide our brains and energetic bodies to what we are trying to accomplish. In many of these rituals, you may be working through something painful or celebrating something joyful. Channeling that pain or joy into your magick will help make the magick more effective, because emotions are energy and energy is a requirement for making magick work. You have to have fuel in the tank for the car to go! It's also important to have time where you give yourself permission to feel things that may be uncomfortable, and these rituals can provide that. While a ritual is no substitute for mental healthcare, taking time to sit with and let emotions flow through you is good, and not something all of us are accustomed to doing with regularity. A ritual can give you time and space to process your feelings. If you anticipate a ritual will be emotionally intense, it's a good idea to talk to a trusted magickal mentor, clergy member, or mental health professional ahead of time and have a plan for how to comfort yourself afterward, including checking in with them or with a trusted friend.

CHOOSING THE SPACE

Your ritual space should be private, quiet, and free from distractions. If you live with other people, you will want to make sure they know not to disturb you until you come out of ritual, or you may want to schedule your ritual for a time when they are away. If you don't have control over the ambient noise level around your ritual space (e.g., if your ritual space has thin walls or is in a noisy area), put on some headphones and a chill playlist of instrumental music to help keep you from getting distracted during ritual. Make sure your ritual space has enough light to read by if you'll be reading parts of the ritual from the book or a piece of paper.

✦ ✦ ✦

A rite of passage ritual is an important event, so it's critical to give it plenty of forethought. Spending some time figuring out the partners and energies, timing, materials, sensory and emotional energies, and location of your ritual ahead of time will help it run smoothly. Once you've got all the details sorted, then you're ready to perform your ritual.

Chapter 2
PERFORMING THE RITUAL

When you've chosen your partners and energies, figured out when to perform your ritual, gathered your ritual materials, and chosen your ritual space, it's time to focus on the ritual itself. Just prior to the ritual, you'll want to arrange and cleanse the space, energetically cleanse yourself, and ground and center yourself.

ARRANGE THE SPACE

Set up the ritual materials ahead of time. Decorate your altar with any magickal items or decorations you want to include. Unless noted otherwise, make sure all the ritual materials are accessible inside where you plan to cast the circle.

Be careful in choosing the place where you'll put anything that needs to be set on fire (candles and incense)—be sure it isn't near any curtains, directly on carpet, on any wobbly surfaces, or near anything that could easily catch fire. Make sure it is out of reach of pets. Know where the nearest fire extinguisher is, just in case, and never leave anything burning unattended.

Have your journal or phone nearby for jotting down or recording your thoughts immediately after ritual. Put your phone on airplane mode so notifications don't distract you during or immediately after the ritual.

ENERGETIC CLEANSING AND GROUNDING

We are constantly surrounded by different types of energy, and some energies are less conducive to ritual. Think about the types of energy you encounter as you go through your day. If you encounter someone with road rage as you drive, some of that angry *ick* may stick to you. If you have a serious conversation with a partner, the heaviness of that energy can stick around in the space and with each of you for a while after the conversation. Regular energetic cleansing of yourself and your space is good spiritual hygiene, helps your magick be more effective, and makes you and your space feel better.

Cleansing the Space

You want your ritual space to be a blank slate, ready for your magickal work, so it's important to cleanse the space just before doing your ritual. First, I recommend physically cleaning the space—picking up clutter, dusting, and vacuuming or sweeping and mopping. Physical cleaning adds to the effectiveness of energetic cleansing.

There are many ways to energetically cleanse a space, enough to fill an entire book. I encourage you to use whatever method resonates with your own magickal practice and whatever you do regularly, but if this concept is new to you, here are some ideas for how to do energetic cleansing. Whichever way you choose to cleanse, the important thing is to *not skip this step*.

Sacred Smoke

Incense is a traditional energetic cleansing technique. You simply light a stick of incense, a charcoal with loose incense in a censer, or a bundle of dried herbs and walk around your space while carefully spreading the smoke around using your hand or a paper or feather fan. Hold in your mind the intent to cleanse the space. There are certain types of incense and herbs that are particularly suitable for cleansing, including cedar (any variety), frankincense (*Boswellia carteri*), myrrh (*Commiphora myrrha*), and rosemary (*Rosmarinus officinalis*). Some cleansing herbs align with specific modalities of magickal practice (e.g., white sage with Indigenous American traditions), so it's useful to check to see which may be most suitable for the way you practice. Also check to make sure the incense or herbs are ethically sourced, and practice good fire safety when burning anything.

Besom

A besom is a sacred broom used for energetic cleansing. To use a besom, sweep just above the floor in a counterclockwise direction, holding in your mind the intent to energetically cleanse the space and move unwanted energies out. Sweep all the way to the exit of the ritual space.

Sound

Energy is vibration, and sound creates vibrations that can elevate and eliminate unwanted energetic patterns. If you have a set of bells of different pitches, ring them while moving around your ritual space clockwise, starting with the bell with the lowest pitch and working your way to the bell with the highest pitch, holding in your mind the intention to cleanse the space. You can also use singing bowls for this purpose in a similar way.

Salt Water Spray

Mix a small amount of salt with water, put it in a spray bottle, and spray it around the space, holding in your mind the intent to energetically cleanse the space and move unwanted energies out. You can also boil the water ahead of time with salt, cleansing herbs, and a bit of lemon or vinegar, if you wish. Be sure to let it cool to room temperature before pouring it into a spray bottle.

ENERGETIC CLEANSING OF SELF AND RITUAL MATERIALS

Another component of preparing for ritual is cleansing the self and your materials. Cleansing yourself helps you get into ritual headspace, serves as a self-blessing, and reminds you that you are divine. For each ritual, you can do this one of several ways:

+ Shower or bathe before ritual
+ Waft sacred smoke over yourself (which represents air and fire) and dab salt water on yourself (which represents earth and water)
+ Wash your hands with intent, focusing on the four elements present in the water: minerals in the water are earth, the air around the water is air, the water is water, and the heat of the water is fire.

These are just three examples; if you regularly use a different self-cleansing or purification method, use that instead.

You should also cleanse any objects to be used in ritual, though not every single ritual material requires cleansing. Art supplies do not need to be cleansed, for example, but you should energetically cleanse anything that absorbs or emits strong energies, like crystals or candles. You can use sacred smoke or sound to cleanse these items, or leave them in sunlight for a day, though I wouldn't recommend the sunlight method for candles, as they may melt.

Salt water can be used to cleanse some objects to be used in ritual, but be careful when using salt water to cleanse anything metal or any crystals, because some types of crystals become toxic in water (e.g., malachite) or can be corroded by salt (e.g., hematite).[15] If you'd like to use salt water for crystal cleansing, look up the crystal's properties first and see how it reacts to salt and water to be sure it won't become toxic or damaged.

If you have tools you regularly use, like an athame or wand, you may want to cleanse them on some regular cadence, but it's not a good idea to cleanse them before every ritual, as it may wear off the magick you've put into them.

Ground and Center

After you've finished energetically cleansing the space, yourself, and any ritual materials, spend a few minutes grounding and centering. Grounding and centering is a method of calming your mind, bringing you into a state of mindfulness in the present moment, and connecting with your body in the here-and-now. It's important to ground and center prior to magickal work for a few reasons:

- It serves as a transition between the preparation of the ritual into the ritual itself, one that helps you move from your mundane persona into your magickal persona.
- It puts you in a calm emotional state, ready to focus and connect with the energies of the ritual.
- It helps you tune in with your body and become aware of your energy in this present moment.

There are a number of grounding and centering meditations available. Here is one you can try. Though it involves connecting with the earth below and sky above, you can do this meditation indoors.

---

15. Ceida Uilyc, "How to Cleanse Hematite Crystals," AllCrystal, accessed February 24, 2024, https://www.allcrystal.com/articles/how-to-cleanse-hematite/.

Grounding and Centering Meditation

Stand if you are able, or sit up with your feet on the floor. Close your eyes.

Take three deep belly breaths, letting your breath out slowly each time. Feel any stress, tension, or worries slip off of you like you're gently slipping off a backpack. You can return to them later if needed.

On your next inhale, feel the warm, solid energy from the earth beneath you rise up through your feet. On each subsequent inhalation, feel the energy rise up further in your body: through your calves, your knees, your thighs, your hips, your belly, your chest, your arms, your neck, and your head.

Now, on another inhale, feel the cool, airy energy of the sky above descending down through the crown of your head. On each subsequent inhalation, feel the energy descend a bit further down your body, and as it descends, feel it intermingle with the earth energy that rose up through you earlier. The energy from the sky travels down through your head, your neck, your arms, your chest, your belly, your hips, your thighs, your calves, and your feet.

Take a deep breath and become aware of the two energies intermingling within you, connecting you to the above and below.

Now find the point within you that feels like your center of consciousness. This point changes frequently, and there are no right answers. Let it freely drift around within yourself until it finds a spot where it feels balanced. Breathe into that space, and let that breath go.

When you are ready, open your eyes.

Grounding after Ritual

It's also important to ground *after* ritual, which may take the form of repeating the grounding and centering meditation, but more commonly takes the form of eating and drinking, which helps you reconnect to your physical body and the physical world. Though you may experience a pleasant energetic rush during ritual that continues afterward, it's important to bring yourself back into the here and now fairly soon once the ritual is complete. Some practitioners get so hooked on the high of working with the numinous that they use it as an escape, which isn't healthy and can lead people to struggle getting through day-to-day life. The gift of incarnation, of being in our physical bodies here on this plane, is what allows us to experience the joys of material existence and to make a difference for ourselves and others, so it's wise to practice mindfulness and being conscious of and connected to your physical form.

CREATE A RITUAL CONTAINER (SACRED SPACE)

Each ritual will contain instructions for creating an energetic container for the ritual, also known as sacred space. By creating an energetic container for the ritual, you can more easily condense and direct the energy you raise. You can think of the energy raised in ritual like steam coming from a tea kettle. If steam is released freely outdoors, it won't do much: it will simply disperse. However, if you direct that steam through a confined space, like a steam engine, the steam is held together tightly enough that it creates motion and heats things up. You want to make sure your magick has a place to be focused so your raised energy doesn't dissipate.

While the ritual container keeps your magick focused inside, it also serves the important function of keeping unwanted spirits and energies *out* of your ritual space. An energetic container acts much like a bouncer at a nightclub—keeping outside anything you didn't invite.

There are several different methods of creating a ritual container within this book. In some rituals, it is a guided meditation while sitting still, creating an energetic bubble around yourself. In others, particularly group rituals, a more formal method is used, often including someone walking around the ritual space while tracing an energetic line with their finger, a wand, or an athame to form a circle-shaped boundary around the ritual space. The key to creating any ritual container is that you must believe it is there, even though you can't see it with your physical eyes. You must believe it is protecting you and containing your magick. If this is a new process to you, don't panic: just like any skill, the more you do it, the easier it becomes, and that includes the *belief* part of the equation. You may find it helpful to end your ritual container creation by saying, with confidence, out loud, "The circle is cast," "I am in sacred space," or a similar phrase that resonates for you.

Entire books have been written on casting sacred space—*Casting Sacred Space* by Ivo Dominguez Jr. is particularly good—so there's much more to learn than I can impart in this small space. But here is a small primer on how to do it.

CREATING A RITUAL CONTAINER

Creating a ritual container involves focusing your mind clearly on what you want to do, feeling and visualizing the energy flow through you, and directing that energy to create a container. All of this is easier to do if you ground and center immediately beforehand.

1. **Focus your mind clearly:** Breathe. Quiet your mind to the best of your ability. Think about what you are trying to do—not for the whole ritual, but just for the creation of the container. Think about making a room, a wall, a bubble—whatever visualization works for you. Picture it as clearly as you can.

2. **Feel and visualize the energy flowing through you:** Breathe. Quiet your mind to the best of your ability. Focus on the feeling of your own body. Feel how your whole body responds to each inhale and exhale. When you want to move energy into yourself, breathe in. When you want to push energy out, breathe out.

3. **Direct that energy:** Now, breathe in and feel and visualize energy drawing into you from beneath your feet, up through your body, into your arms, and down into your dominant hand. Point your finger, and as you exhale, push that energy in your hand out through your fingertip, visualizing it pouring out as a bright line while you move in a circle around your ritual space. It may help to purse your lips a little so the air comes out more slowly and forcefully as you exhale. You don't have to do this all on a single exhale; pause to breathe in, drawing up more energy, then breathe out and continue moving as you push more energy out.

4. **Focus:** Know that this energetic circle you are creating is a definitive boundary between the inside and outside of your ritual circle and that it will contain the energy that you raise during the ritual.

5. **Connect it up:** Remember to connect your line of energy back to the beginning so it forms a complete circle.

Congratulations! You've just cast a circle!

I included a variety of types of ritual containers and casting methods within this book for two reasons: First, I wanted to show folks who are newer to creating ritual containers that there are a number of different ways to do so with varying levels of complexity. Second, I wanted to design some specific ritual containers that resonate with the work of each ritual, adding to the ritual's power. However, if you already have a defined and preferred method of circle casting you're comfortable with, you may use your own method instead.

DECLARE THE INTENT OF THE RITUAL

When you declare the intent of the ritual, you are focusing the minds and intents of those physically or energetically present—yourself, your own higher consciousness, and any helper spirits, ancestors, or deities—toward your goal. It's important to say the statement of intent out loud and with conviction. You are telling the universe, "This is what is going to happen. This is my Will." Be confident. Declare it. That also goes for anything you say out loud during a ritual.

Depending on your specific goals for a ritual, you may want to add to or change the statement of intent to focus on your particular goals. Just keep it under a few sentences so it's easy for all those present, both human and spirit, to understand.

WELCOME IN SPIRITS

If you choose to involve spirits—helper spirits, ancestors, or divine beings—in your ritual, this is your opportunity to welcome them and ask for their help. If you choose not to work with any spirits or divine beings, skip this step.

In each ritual, I've provided sample welcoming language using one of the deities in the Partners and Energies section. Unless you're working with the deity I suggest, customize the welcome to the deities or spirits you are involving in the ritual by replacing the suggested deity's name and epithets (commonly used descriptive words for that deity or spirit) with your chosen deity's or spirit's name and epithets.

Each welcome statement includes a specific request for what you'd like the deities or spirits to do in your ritual. Sometimes you'll just ask for their presence, guidance, and protection; sometimes you'll ask for something more specific if they have a particular role to play in the ritual. You may customize this statement to better align with your practice and the focus of your personal ritual.

Many of the rituals include a separate welcome for the queer ancestors or a specific subset of queer ancestors. You may replace this with a call to a specific queer ancestor if there is one you feel a strong connection to or feel would be particularly helpful for that ritual. If you are not immediately comfortable working with queer ancestors, I encourage you to give it a try and see how it impacts your practice. However, if you are strongly averse to ancestor veneration, you may skip this step. For rituals that have a role for queer ancestors to play, replace them with a deity or helper spirit that better aligns with your practice.

Again, be sure you say the welcome out loud with strength and conviction. As you welcome them, fill yourself with the desire to have these helper spirits, deities, ancestors, and other divine beings present for and helping with your ritual.

RAISE ENERGY OR CONSCIOUSNESS

The real nuts and bolts of a ritual focuses on raising and directing energy. Energy is the fuel of magick, and when you give it a destination, that's how you can get things to manifest. You need both energy and a place to put it in order to accomplish the purpose of the ritual. You can't direct energy without raising it first, and it's rather pointless to raise energy and then not do anything with it. These two steps are the focal point of the ritual.

Raising energy can include actions like lighting a candle, playing music, clapping, singing, chanting, drumming, or dancing. These physical actions increase the amount of energy in your ritual space. The increase in energy may feel subtle, especially if you're doing something like lighting a candle, or it may feel very buzzy and intense, especially if you are dancing or drumming.

In some of the rituals in this book, you're invited to play prerecorded music. It's wise to have a backup plan (singing, chanting, or clapping should suffice), as electronics can sometimes misbehave in ritual circles and may not work as expected. Also, if you're using your phone to play music, download the music ahead of time and then put your phone on airplane mode so you don't get distracted by notifications while you're in ritual. If you're using a computer to play music, close out of any programs that create pop-up or audio notifications.

Instead of doing a physical action to raise energy, you may instead raise your consciousness, which also raises the energy needed to perform magick by stirring emotion and raising your personal vibration. Raising consciousness usually involves a guided meditation of some kind. Many of the included rituals contain a guided meditation component. Most of them are short and simple, but for some of the longer or more complex ones, you may want to record yourself reading the meditation aloud ahead of time and play it back for yourself during ritual. If you do this, remember while recording to go slowly and take plenty of time to pause and let yourself explore during the meditation. A good guide is when there's an opportunity to converse with a spirit, consider an idea, or explore something, add a pause of at least one to two minutes before resuming reading the meditation aloud.

Alternatively, you can jot down key words to remember on a piece of paper to have as a cheat sheet to keep with you in ritual to consult if you get lost.

FOCUS, DIRECT, OR RELEASE ENERGY

Once you've raised energy, it's time to put it someplace. This is literally *where the magick happens*. The oven is preheated, and now we're going to bake a cake!

Focusing, directing, and releasing energy is when we send the energy we've raised in the previous step toward our goal for the ritual. This is different for every ritual. For some, you will be pouring energy into a specific item, like a talisman or crystal, to charge it with a specific intent. In others, you will be declaring something, claiming your sovereignty, or cutting energetic ties with someone. And in others, you will be charging and blessing yourself with energy you need. Whether you put the energy into an object or yourself, this moment requires focus. Take a breath, clear your mind, and focus on exactly what you want to have happen. Speak your desire aloud if the ritual calls for it or if you feel so moved. Do each step slowly and carefully. When you've completed this step, you may also want to pause to feel the important work you've accomplished. Taking a moment for gratitude or processing is always a good idea.

CLOSE THE RITUAL

It's important for your own mind and those people and spirits gathered to know when the ritual has concluded. First, thank and say goodbye to the spirits who assisted you. I've provided words you can use to thank these beings in each ritual, but you'll want to customize them for the specific deities and helper spirits you choose to work with, as you did when you welcomed them in. You may also spontaneously add additional words of gratitude when you get to this part in the ritual.

Next, release the energetic container you created for the ritual. Because I believe strongly that magickal practitioners have the opportunity to re-enchant the earth, I do not include instructions to *banish* a circle by taking it down counterclockwise, but instead I instruct you to *open* a circle by pulling the energy back through you and into the earth, clockwise, so the energy is gently returned instead of being banished. If you have a regular practice you're more comfortable with for opening or dismissing a circle, you may use that instead, as long as it matches with the way you created the ritual container at the beginning.

WHAT TO DO AFTER RITUAL

Some rituals have specific instructions for what to do with the ritual materials afterward. Unless it says otherwise, you may reuse these materials for future rituals. In some cases, you will be asked to burn ritual items in sacred fire. To create a sacred fire, simply bless a fire in a firepit or fireplace. Ask it to energetically, as well as physically, destroy the items you are about to offer it, and then toss them in. If you don't have easy access to a fireplace or firepit, save these items in a special jar you designate for this purpose, and destroy them in a sacred fire when you have the opportunity to do so. In a pinch, you can burn these objects in a heavy cooking pot or other fireproof vessel in your home, being careful of fire safety in the same way I mentioned in the ritual setup section.

The psychological and magickal impact of a rite of passage ritual is not limited to the time the ritual is taking place, or even the day the ritual is taking place. You may feel the impact of the energy of the ritual in the days leading up to it, and possibly for months afterward. These rituals are intended to help make shifts in your life, and if they are effective, they will do so. And shifts in your life sometimes bring forth previously repressed emotions, and sometimes, unexpected impacts in other areas of your life.

To that end, I strongly recommend that you pair these rituals with a plan for support afterward. For starters, I encourage you to set up regular check-ins for processing with another person. If you have the privilege of access to mental health care, I highly recommend working with a therapist. Realizing that isn't possible for everyone, and that not all mental health care professionals are accepting of witchcraft, if you have a trusted mentor, spiritual leader, or empathetic friend, you may be able to have some regular conversations with them about your progress integrating and processing your rite of passage. Though these types of interactions do not have the same benefits and structure as therapy, they are a better support option than keeping everything to yourself indefinitely.

Be gentle with yourself. Take some time to breathe, to experience quiet, to listen to your body and your heart in the weeks following the ritual. Ask questions of yourself, but also take time to simply allow thoughts, images, and words to arise through meditation, journeying, or simply pausing.

The Follow Through

What life changes should you expect after a rite of passage ritual? If you've put a specific intent into your working, it likely will not manifest immediately, and it may not manifest at all if you don't do work in the mundane world to support it. For a magickal working intended to help you get a new job, for example, you would need to support it by putting in applications or sending out resumes. For a rite of passage ritual, the mundane work to support it may be less obvious. Here are some things I recommend, both leading up to and following your ritual, to increase its effectiveness and potency:

Mindfulness Practice

If you do not already have a regular mindfulness or meditation practice, a great time to start one would be during the time surrounding a rite of passage. *Mindfulness* is the practice of being fully present in the moment, without chasing ideas, thinking about the past or the future, or worrying. You can weave moments of mindfulness throughout your daily life. *Meditation* is a practice of quieting your mind or focusing on one particular sensation, like your breath, for a certain period of time. The benefits of each practice increase with regular repetition.

For those resistant to the idea of meditation or who have struggled with it in the past, know that meditation does not have to be sitting still with your eyes closed. Walking in nature mindfully, without looking at your phone, is a form of meditation. Sitting with your eyes open and focusing on your breath for a minute is a form of meditation. Yoga is a form of meditation if you are doing the poses slowly and mindfully. It may be easier to commit to a regular meditation practice for a limited time—perhaps for the week leading up to your rite of passage and the month after. There are a lot of helpful apps available that can ease you into a regular meditation practice.

Meditation and mindfulness in any form add some spiritual listening time to your life, creating a margin where your higher self and helper spirits or divine beings have the opportunity to talk to you, even if it's only for a few minutes a week. As you approach and recover from a rite of passage, you want to open yourself to your higher self for guidance and information.

Journal

If you do not already have a regular journaling practice, again, a great time to start, or at least develop a temporary practice, would be during the time surrounding a rite of passage. Journaling doesn't have to be done with pen and paper; you can record yourself speaking, use a speech-to-text function with a note-taking app on your phone, or even draw or create art that can express your feelings and help you process. The point is that you should get the stuff *inside* your head *outside* of it.

I encourage you to journal immediately after the ritual is complete, as the experiences in rituals can fade rather quickly, and you may wish to revisit the experience later. Journaling your feelings leading up to the ritual and in the weeks and months following the ritual can also bring new insights and help process your experience on a deeper level.

Buy Yourself a Gift

Sometimes you may be inspired to buy yourself a gift to honor your rite of passage. I think this is a great idea, especially if the gift to yourself is something directly related to the outcomes you hoped to see in your life after the rite of passage ritual. For example, if you were to follow your gender exploration ritual (page 52) with a trip to the thrift store to buy a gender-affirming piece of clothing, that would be entirely appropriate.

MAKING OFFERINGS

Finally, following any of these rituals, particularly the ones where you call to the queer ancestors, it would be appropriate to make a queer ancestor offering. The best way to thank our queer ancestors is to strengthen the queer community, and you can support the energy you have raised and directed in ritual by paying it forward and helping others.

On the day of the ritual or shortly thereafter, consider donating to a queer nonprofit or taking an advocacy action on behalf of queer causes by writing a letter or calling your elected officials on a particular issue. In a way, doing so gives the queer ancestors the opportunity to keep helping our community even after they've departed this plane. If you make a donation, you can state it's in honor of any named ancestors you invited to your ritual. If you write a letter, you can note that you are inspired by the tireless efforts of those named ancestors. This helps keep the ancestors' spirits alive and thriving, and will help them be more inclined to continue helping you in the future.

There's a list of great organizations (see page 205) you can donate to and learn from.

◆ ◆ ◆

The rituals in this book are written with a consistent set of steps. The more you practice rituals in this format, the easier they become to perform and, eventually, to write. Each step does something specific to ensure the ritual is effective and the magick you create is as potent as possible. If you are new to writing and performing rituals, I hope this book will give you a solid foundation for customizing these rituals in ways that are authentic to you, and give you the tools you need to create rituals of your own.

PART 2:
THE RITUALS

Chapter 3
PERSONAL RITES FOR IDENTITY EXPLORATION AND AFFIRMATION

A big part of being queer is exploring and coming to new understandings of your identity. Queer people are not the only ones to experiment with our identities and how we express them, but it's certainly a defining part of the queer experience to test, and at some point affirm, your identity. Even if you've known your gender or sexuality since you were very young, there are always going to be moments of realization of your difference from the cisgender, heterosexual norms portrayed in popular culture. Your gender and sexuality may also evolve over time and feel different to you at different times of your life, leading you to affirm and integrate these new understandings.

Most of the rituals in this section are personal rites, meant to be done alone, to give you the breathing room to explore and declare to yourself *who you are* without fear of how others see you. Some can be adapted to a group setting, but it's important that you feel comfortable with the group and won't be distracted worrying about how long you spend doing a pathworking or how you express emotions during the ritual.

SEXUALITY EXPLORATION RITUAL

Popular television and movies often portray the story of someone coming out as gay, lesbian, bisexual, pansexual, asexual, or any other sexual identity as a secret held by a person that they finally decide to tell people. And then they're out! A happy ending, right? What those stories often *don't* show is the time that person spent wondering if their sexual identity might be different from what they thought or what other people assumed it was. They also don't show a person changing their mind, or shifting their understanding of themselves, over time.

What if you came out as gay five years ago, but now you find yourself attracted to someone of a different gender? What if you hadn't ever considered whether you might be asexual, but suddenly it's all you can think about? What if you thought you were straight, but now you find yourself attracted to a nonbinary or gender-queer person? What if you thought you were monogamous but are coming to realize polyamory is a better fit for you?

Many people experience a fluid sexuality over the course of their life, one that evolves and shifts over time in subtle or dramatic ways. For some, these explorations may be low stress and go on for quite some time. For others, exploring one's sexuality can bring up all kinds of feelings like confusion, impostor syndrome, isolation, or even a full-blown identity crisis.

In this ritual, we create a meditative space for your explorations and a way to detach yourself from external pressures for a bit. This ritual doesn't aim to give you immediate answers, but can be a stepping stone toward clarity. By meditating on our feelings of love and passion, we can begin to better recognize those feelings as they take the shape of our sexuality. The addition of divination can help point the way if you're feeling lost.

Any insights you glean from this ritual are for you to do with as you wish. You may choose to share with others or not. You may decide you need more time to think about things before you take on a new identity. All of that is okay. It's important to go into this ritual with an open mind that is not focused on what others think.

If you find yourself experiencing panic or great discomfort during this ritual, it's okay to end it at any time. You may come back to it later if you choose to. If you experience mental or emotional distress during or after this ritual, please be gentle with yourself. Speak with a trusted friend or mental health professional; take some time and space to both feel the feelings and allow yourself some comfort media, snacks, deep breaths, cuddles with pets or plushies, or whatever else helps you feel safe.

PARTNERS AND ENERGIES

The following partners and energies are particularly well-suited for this ritual's task.

PARTNERS

- **Celtic:** Aengus
- **Egyptian:** Ma'at, Set, Horus, Isis
- **Greek:** Dionysus, Aphrodite, Eros (used as an example in the following version), Pan, Apollo, Athena (if exploring asexuality)
- **Norse:** Freyja, Freyr, Odinn

ANCESTORS

A call to queer ancestors is included in this rite. You may call whichever queer ancestors you wish, whether they are the stream of power of all the queer people who have existed before you, specific queer people from history, people with a specific sexuality, or queer people from your own lineage.

ENERGIES

There are a few different astrological correspondences you can work with here, depending on how you're feeling about things. If you're really in a headspace where lust is confusing, use Mars. If you're wondering more about the romantic side of things, use Venus. And if you're really just not sure because everything is kind of a confusing muddle, try the Moon to uncover what is hidden.

- **Planets:** Moon (to uncover what is hidden), Venus (for romance), Mars (for sex/lust)
- **Qabala:** Yesod, Netzach, Geburah

- **Elements:** Water (emotions) or fire (passion/sex)
- **Tarot:** The Moon, Page of Wands

RECOMMENDED TIMING

Performing this ritual on any of the following days or at any of the following times will add power to this working.

- **Days of the week:** Monday (if working with the Moon), Tuesday (if working with Mars), or Friday (if working with Venus)
- **Planetary hours:** Moon, Mars, or Venus
- **Moon phase:** Dark

RITUAL MATERIALS

- An unscented red jar candle
- Lighter or matches
- Jasmine or sandalwood essential oil
- A very soft blanket or sweater
- A divination method, e.g., a deck of tarot or oracle cards or a set of runes
- About 30 minutes of evocative drum music on a computer or smartphone, and headphones if needed
- *Optional:* a wand or athame, whichever is the tool for fire within your practice

Note: Remember when bringing music into ritual to download the music beforehand. Put your phone on airplane mode or close out any noisy programs on your computer so you aren't distracted by notifications during the ritual.

SENSORY AND EMOTIONAL ENERGIES TO TIE IN

There's an interesting tension in this rite, because we simultaneously want to detach from our emotions but also feel them deeply. Think of it like putting your emotions in a jar and then holding them up to examine them. We will be focusing on scent and tactile sensations in this ritual to key into our own sensuality.

Ritual Preparation

Tidy up and then cleanse your working space with sacred smoke, a besom, or whatever space-clearing practice resonates with you. Set up your altar with the ritual materials. Put the blanket or sweater near where you will be sitting during this ritual. Set up a chair if you don't want to sit on the floor for the meditation portion.

Ground and center yourself. Wash your hands with awareness of the sacredness of the water and all four elements present in the water, or use another purification method of your choosing.

The Ritual

You will now create your ritual container. Face east. Take three deep breaths slowly. Breathe in through your nose and out through your mouth. Let your worries melt away, and feel yourself begin to focus on the magickal work that is about to take place.

Visualize or feel yourself pulling bright blue, brilliant energy from the earth and sky into yourself as you inhale, then pushing that energy out through the tip of your wand, athame, or the index finger on your dominant hand as you exhale. Move in a clockwise circle around your ritual space, beginning and ending in the east, visualizing a sharp, crisp line coming out of your wand, athame, or finger and forming a circle. Once it is formed, exhale once again and visualize flipping the circle around vertically until it forms a sphere.

Declare the Intent of the Ritual

Say: "In this ritual, I will examine my desires in order to bring clarity to my evolving sexuality. I will seek guidance through divination. I will remember that I am loved and that I am a divine being."

Welcome in Spirits

Call to your chosen deity using their epithets. For example, say: "Eros, god of love, I call to you this day to aid me in revealing my inner truths amid possibilities as I explore my sexuality. Guide me and help me come to a new understanding of myself. Hail and welcome."

Call to the queer ancestors. Say: "To the queer ancestors, to [name(s)], I call you and ask that you join my rite today. Please bring me guidance and wisdom from your experience. Hail and welcome."

If you wish to welcome in any other deities, allies, and helper spirits, please do so in your own words.

Raise Energy and Consciousness

Breathe in the scent of the oil as you drip one drop of it on the top of the unlit jar candle, away from the wick, then spread it around the top of the candle with your finger to distribute the oil, being careful not to get any on the wick. (If you have sensitive skin, use a carrier oil like olive oil.) Say: "May this scent awaken the powers of the sensual within me."

As you light the candle, say: "May this flame guide me on my journey inward."

Sit down, putting the blanket or sweater in your lap. Feel its softness. Take a moment to enjoy the feeling of touching it.

Begin playing the drum music on your computer or smartphone, and put on your headphones if you're using them. Breathe deeply from your diaphragm, and feel the drums resonate within your body. Close your eyes if you wish, or focus on the flame of the candle—whichever brings you into a deeper meditative state.

Feel your consciousness drift toward your heart. Become aware of the feeling of your heart beating. Call up the emotion of love and sit in that feeling for a while. It does not have to be romantic love, though you can focus on that if you prefer. You may end up focusing on the love you have for one or more individuals, and that is okay. Try to focus on the feeling of love without getting caught up in anxiety or replaying past events though. What does love feel like in your body?

+ Does your heart race?
+ Do you feel warmth spreading throughout your chest?
+ Do you blush?
+ What other sensations are you aware of?

Whatever it feels like is okay; there are no wrong answers here. When the feeling, or absence of feeling, is clear, imagine yourself capturing it in a bubble or a jar and stepping back to examine it. What does it look like or sound like?

After a few moments, step back into that feeling by pulling that bubble or jar back into your heart, and note if it feels any different than it did before.

Now feel your consciousness drift downward to your sacral region, the lowest part of your abdomen and genitals. Become aware of any sensations there. Call up the emotion of sexual attraction, desire, or arousal, if that is something you experience, and sit in that feeling for a while. If you do not experience sexual attraction or arousal, simply become aware of the sensations in your body when you focus on this part of your physical self. If sexual attraction or arousal is something you *do* experience, you may end up focusing on the feeling of sexual attraction you have for one or more individuals, and that is okay. Try to focus on the *feeling* of arousal or attraction without spinning out into replaying past events or fantasies though. Do you experience attraction or arousal, and if so, where in your body do you feel it? Focus on your sacral region at first, then expand your focus to the rest of your body.

+ Does your heart race?
+ Does your face flush?
+ Do your lips feel warm?
+ Does the light feel brighter on your eyelids?
+ What other sensations are you aware of?

Whatever it feels like is okay; there are no wrong answers here. When the feeling, or absence of feeling, is clear, imagine yourself capturing it in a bubble or a jar and stepping back to examine it. What does it look like or sound like?

After a few moments, step back into that feeling by pulling that bubble or jar back into your sacral region, and note if it feels any differently than it did before.

Ask for Guidance

Now call upon the deity or spirit(s) you invited to the ritual. For example, say: "Eros, I seek your guidance. Through the realms of inner chaos, help me find that which is true for me in this time in my life."

Allow the deity or spirit(s) to guide you. They may engage you in dialogue, they may show you something hidden, you may go on a journey with them, they may tell you some things you hadn't considered or weren't willing to consider. Have an open mind and listen.

Next, call upon the queer ancestors you invited to the ritual. Say: "[Queer ancestors or their name(s)], I seek your guidance. Help me find that which is authentic, that which is my inner truth in this moment."

Allow the ancestors to guide you. They may engage you in dialogue, they may show you something hidden, you may go on a journey with them, they may tell you some things you hadn't considered or weren't willing to consider. Have an open mind and listen.

When you feel your meditation and your work with the ancestors has reached its conclusion, turn off the music if you wish to do so, then shuffle your cards or mix up your runes and draw three of them with intention.

As you draw the first one, focus on the idea of how you've understood your sexuality in the past. Place it on the left.

As you draw the second one, focus on the idea of how you understand your sexuality now. Place it to the right of the first one.

As you draw the third one, focus on the idea of how you may understand your sexuality in the future. Place it to the right of the second one.

Contemplate what you drew for a few moments. If you would like more clarity, ask for guidance from the divine being you invited into the ritual and the queer ancestors.

When you feel you understand the message, or when you come to a point where you want to set it aside and think more on it later, thank the divine being and ancestors for their aid.

Focus Energy

Gaze at the candle. Smell the oil and feel the soft blanket once again, appreciating the scent and texture. Breathe in deeply, and as you do, pull the energy from the candle flame into yourself, and feel it spread throughout your physical and subtle bodies. Feel the fire within you grow brighter, and remember that your sexuality is a sacred gift and you are the sovereign of it. Your body is your own, and you are empowered and blessed to enjoy both solitary and consensual partnered sensual pleasures. Express gratitude for this gift in your own words, either aloud or to yourself.

Thanks and Farewell

It is time to say your goodbyes to any spirits who attended the ritual. First, thank your chosen deity using their epithets. For example, say: "Eros, god of love, I thank you for aiding me in revealing my inner truths in my exploration of my sexuality. I bid you hail and farewell."

Next, bid farewell to the queer ancestors. Say: "Queer ancestors, [name(s)], I thank you for your guidance in my ritual today. I bid you hail and farewell."

Using your own words, say farewell to any other divine beings or helper spirits you called in to the ritual.

Close the Ritual

Blow out the candle.

Visualize the sphere you cast folding back down into a flat circle. Starting in the east, using your wand, athame, or index finger, draw the energy of the circle back through yourself and into the earth, moving clockwise around your ritual space.

Post Ritual

Remember to ground and center yourself again, either with meditation or by eating or drinking something. Journal, draw, or record yourself speaking about your experience while it's fresh in your mind. Take a photo of the cards or runes you drew, or write them down in your journal, for further consideration in the days ahead. More information may come to you in dreams or meditation.

You may reuse the candle for any future workings related to personal exploration, sensuality, sexuality, or passion.

GENDER EXPLORATION RITUAL

Everyone can benefit from taking some time to explore their gender, even if you are cisgender (fully identifying with the gender you were assigned at birth). We get so many messages about what our gender is from external sources—family, friends, media—but most of us don't spend a ton of time venturing inward to discover what we believe about our own gender and what makes us feel like the gender we are.

For those who are considering whether they might be nonbinary, transgender, genderfluid, or any other flavor of genderqueer, this ritual can help bring some clarity to your explorations. Do not go into this ritual expecting immediate, clear answers, but consider this ritual a step on the way to better understanding things, a tool to jostle loose feelings that may be hidden or stuck. Using the tool of free-writing combined with meditation, we can discover new things about ourselves.

Gender identity (how you *feel* your gender) and gender expression (how you *show* your gender to the world) are two different things, and you may find yourself exploring one more than the other in this ritual, regardless of your intention. That's okay! You can certainly repeat this ritual as many times as you need to gain additional insights.

If you find yourself experiencing panic or great discomfort during this ritual, it's okay to end it at any time. You may come back to it later if you choose to. If you experience mental or emotional distress during or after this ritual, please be gentle with yourself. Speak with a trusted friend or mental health professional, take some time and space to both feel the feelings and allow yourself some comfort TV, snacks, deep breaths, cuddles with pets or plushies, or whatever else helps you feel safe.

As part of this ritual, you will journey to your inner temple. This is a modified version of the "Temple of Isis" meditation from *Casting Sacred Space* Ivo Dominguez Jr.[16] This is a space within your own consciousness where you are in full con-

---

16. Ivo Dominguez Jr., *Casting Sacred Space: The Core of All Magickal Work* (San Francisco, CA: Weiser, 2012), 131–34.

trol, where you are the fullest expression of yourself and your power. You may have already constructed an inner temple in previous magickal work, in which case you may journey to it in the ways you've already established. If you haven't previously constructed an inner temple, you will spend some time building it during this ritual.

PARTNERS AND ENERGIES

The following partners and energies are particularly well-suited for this ritual's task.

PARTNERS
+ **Celtic:** The Morrigan, Rhiannon
+ **Egyptian:** Hapi, Asushunamir, Atum, Ma'at
+ **Greek:** Dionysus (used as an example in this ritual), Kybele
+ **Norse:** Loki, Freyja, Freyr, Odinn

ANCESTORS
A call to queer ancestors is included in this rite. You may call whichever queer ancestors you wish, whether they are the stream of power of all the queer people who have existed before you, specific queer people from history, people with a specific gender identity, or queer people from your own lineage.

ENERGIES
+ **Planets:** Moon (for uncovering that which is hidden) or Venus (for how your gender *feels* within you)
+ **Qabala:** Netzach
+ **Elements:** Water (for the fluidity of exploration, flexibility, openness)
+ **Tarot:** The Moon

RECOMMENDED TIMING

Performing this ritual on any of the following days or at any of the following times will add power to this working.

+ **Day of the week:** Monday (for Moon), Friday (for Venus)
+ **Planetary hours:** Moon, Venus

- **Moon phase:** Dark (for uncovering that which is hidden), waxing (for exploration)

Ritual Materials

- A chair
- A notebook or journal
- A pen
- A mirror
- A tea light (or other small candle) and holder
- Lighter or matches
- *Optional:* a comfort object, like a favorite blanket or plushie; a wand or athame, whichever is the tool for fire within your practice

Sensory and Emotional Energies to Tie In

In this ritual, we're working toward the feeling of what fits and feels comfortable to you. If you have clothing that feels particularly good to wear, wear it while doing this ritual to help connect with that energy. If you have a comfort object, like a plushie or favorite blanket, you may include that in the ritual as well.

Ritual Preparation

Tidy up and then cleanse your working space with sacred smoke, a besom, or whatever space-clearing practice resonates with you. Set up your altar with a chair in front of it, and put the notepad and pen on the altar. Prop up the mirror so you can see yourself in it when you sit in the chair, or if the mirror is mounted on the wall or a dresser, make sure you can see it while sitting in the chair and writing. Place the candle and matches or lighter in front of the mirror on a table or stable surface.

Ground and center yourself. Wash your hands with awareness of the sacredness of the water and all four elements present in the water, or use another purification method of your choosing.

THE RITUAL

You will now create your ritual container. Face east. Take three deep breaths slowly. Breathe in through your nose and out through your mouth. Let your worries melt away, and feel yourself begin to focus on the magickal work that is about to take place.

Visualize or feel yourself pulling bright blue, brilliant energy from the earth and sky into yourself as you inhale, then pushing that energy out through the tip of your wand, athame, or the index finger on your dominant hand as you exhale. Move in a clockwise circle around your ritual space, beginning and ending in the east, visualizing a sharp, crisp line coming out of your wand, athame, or finger and forming a circle. Once it is formed, exhale and visualize flipping the circle around vertically until it forms a sphere.

DECLARE THE INTENT OF THE RITUAL

Say the following: "Today, I seek to explore my gender, to learn more about myself and gain clarity, that I may better understand and live my life in a way that is true to myself."

WELCOME IN SPIRITS

Call to your chosen deity using their epithets. For example, say: "Hail Dionysus, you of fluid gender, god of sensual delights and pleasure. I ask that you guide me as I explore my gender identity and expression today. Hail and welcome."

Call to the queer ancestors. Say: "Hail to the queer ancestors, [name(s)], those who have come before me and paved the way for so many people to live in their fullest expression of authentic, queer selfhood. I ask you to join my ritual today and guide me as I explore my gender identity and expression. Hail and welcome."

If you wish to welcome in any other deities, allies, and helper spirits, please do so in your own words.

RAISE CONSCIOUSNESS

Light the candle in front of the mirror and turn off or dim the lights in the room. Sit where you can see yourself in the mirror while writing. Take three deep breaths slowly, and gaze at your reflection. Note without judgment what you see. Take some time to really look at your face in the mirror and notice its details.

If you brought a comfort object into ritual, hold it.

Close your eyes. Visualize a violet swirl of energy spiraling around the middle of your forehead and pointing itself inward, deep into your head. As it does so, feel it pulling your consciousness deeper inside yourself. Feel yourself fall *into* *yourself* and land in your inner temple. Alternatively, use whatever method of traveling to your inner temple that you've previously established.

If this is the first time you've journeyed to your inner temple, take some time to look around. This is your place of power and complete safety: What does it look like? Notice its details. Add things as you see fit. Spend some time here, observing and getting comfortable.

Within your inner temple, find a mirror. If you don't see one, create one. Look at your reflection in the mirror inside your inner temple. You probably look different than you do in the physical realm.

+ What do you notice?
+ Do you like how you look here?
+ Are you able to change your appearance?

Spend some time playing with your appearance.

+ Which of the forms you see look most like how you feel as a person?
+ Which forms feel most comfortable to you?
+ Which are scary but enticing?

As you find forms that particularly speak to you, make a mental note of them.

Say within your inner temple: "I wish to see myself at my most comfortable, as the gender that resonates with my soul."

Now look at the mirror again. What do you see?

When you are ready to depart your inner temple, feel the violet spiral on your forehead gently pull you back from your inner temple into your physical body. (Or use whichever method of travel back from your inner temple you've previously established.) Open your eyes.

Focus and Direct Energy

Look at yourself in the mirror again. Close your eyes and remember what the mirror in your inner temple showed you. Now take the notebook and pen and write *My gender is…*

Continue writing, without stopping, for a few minutes. Write words that come to mind; they don't have to be gender labels. Your gender may be the night sky, it may be the song of a bluebird, or it may be a lot of things you don't have good words for. Don't worry about grammar, spelling, or whether what you're writing feels true or makes sense. Just write freely without thinking. If you find yourself pausing, take a breath, remember what the inner temple showed you, write *My gender is* again, and continue from there.

After a few minutes, stop and read what you've written. Underline anything that surprises you or strikes you in some way. If you wish to continue writing, do so. When you feel you are finished writing and have expressed what you need to today, stop. Remember, you can always come back to this exercise again.

Pause to listen to or have a conversation with the divine entity and the queer ancestors you've invited into the ritual. Ask their thoughts on what you've experienced and written.

Gaze into the candle once more. Feel the warmth of the flame envelop you. Wrap your arms around yourself or, if you brought a comfort object into the ritual, hold it tight. Feel yourself hugging and being hugged. Know that you are loved, that you are worthy of love, that you are a spark of the Divine. Know that you have sovereignty over your body, your identity, and your destiny. Say: "I am myself. I am me. My identity is my own."

Thanks and Farewell

It is time to say your goodbyes to any spirits who attended the ritual. First, thank your chosen deity using their epithets. For example, say: "Dionysus, you of fluid gender and sensual delights, I thank you for your guidance in my ritual today. I bid you hail and farewell."

Bid farewell to the queer ancestors. Say: "Queer ancestors, [name(s)], I thank you for your guidance in my ritual today. I bid you hail and farewell."

Using your own words, say farewell to any other divine beings or helper spirits you called in to the ritual.

Close the Ritual

Blow out the candle.

Visualize the sphere you cast folding back down into a flat circle. Starting in the east, using your wand, athame, or index finger, draw the energy of the circle back through yourself and into the earth, moving clockwise around your ritual space.

Post Ritual

For additional guidance, you may wish to do some divination using a method of your choice immediately following this ritual.

Remember to ground and center yourself again, either with meditation or by eating or drinking something. Journal, draw, or record yourself speaking about your experience while it's fresh in your mind.

Keep the notebook you wrote in and refer back to it in the coming days or weeks. You may wish to repeat this ritual, or at least the freewriting portion of it, to gain additional clarity.

You may reuse the candle for any future rituals related to personal exploration or gender.

SEXUALITY AFFIRMATION RITUAL

There is a point—or sometimes multiple points—in a queer person's journey when they realize they are not heterosexual or heteronormative but something else, whether it's bisexual, pansexual, homosexual, asexual, aromantic, or even polyamorous. Building a ritual to affirm this realization can help you feel more confident when coming out to others about it, should you choose to do so, and may help you crystalize your feelings about it for your own self-awareness.

In this ritual, you will build and bless an altar to honor your sexuality and toast yourself with a decadent treat and beverage.

I invite you to use your tool of fire or water (which may vary, but is typically a wand, athame, or chalice in Western magickal traditions) to cast the circle, which will represent the powers of fire or water in your sexuality. I recommend using a water tool if you want to focus on the emotional and romantic side of your sexuality, and the fire tool if you want to focus on the lust and sexual side of your sexuality. If you don't have dedicated tools to the elements, don't worry; you can use your finger to cast instead.

PARTNERS AND ENERGIES

The following partners and energies are particularly well-suited for this ritual's task. Since sexuality has both romantic and sexual components to it, which one you want to emphasize will determine the types of energies you want to bring in.

PARTNERS
- **Celtic:** Aengus (used as an example in this ritual), the Morrigan, Rhiannon
- **Egyptian:** Ma'at, Set, Horus, Isis
- **Greek:** Dionysus, Aphrodite, Eros, Pan, Apollo, Athena (if affirming asexuality)
- **Norse:** Freyja, Freyr, Odinn

Ancestors

A call to queer ancestors is included in this rite. For this ritual, call in ancestors who share your sexuality, whether they are the stream of power of all the people who share your sexuality, specific people from history, or people from your own lineage.

Energies

+ **Planets:** Venus (for the more romantic side), Mars (for the more sexual side)
+ **Qabala:** Netzach
+ **Elements:** Water (for romance and emotions), fire (for passion and sex)
+ **Tarot:** The Lovers

Recommended Timing

Performing this ritual on any of the following days or at any of the following times will add power to this working.

+ **Days of the week:** Tuesday (for Mars) or Friday (for Venus)
+ **Planetary hours:** Mars or Venus
+ **Moon phase:** Full

Ritual Materials

+ Items to decorate your altar in celebration of your sexuality
+ A red jar candle
+ Lighter or matches
+ A glass of wine or another decadent beverage you enjoy
+ Chocolate or another sweet treat you enjoy
+ *Optional:* a fire or water tool (typically a wand, athame, or chalice)

Note: *In this ritual, you will need items to create an altar for your sexuality. Some ideas include: a pride flag specific to your orientation (purchased, printed, or drawn), photographs of bodies you find attractive, photos of celebrities or ancestors who share your sexual identity, pieces of paper with words to describe your sexuality, fresh flow-*

ers, sex toys, books or magazines related to your sexuality, a photo of yourself, the symbols for Venus or Mars, etc. Get creative!

SENSORY AND EMOTIONAL ENERGIES TO TIE IN

This is a ritual of decadence, affirmation, and celebration. A positive and celebratory mindset will be beneficial for this working.

RITUAL PREPARATION

Tidy up and then cleanse your working space with sacred smoke, a besom, or whatever space-clearing practice resonates with you. Put the red candle on your altar. Set the other ritual materials, including the beverage and sweet treat, near your altar but not on it.

Ground and center yourself. Wash your hands with awareness of the sacredness of the water and all four elements present in the water, or use another purification method of your choosing.

THE RITUAL

You will now create your ritual container. Face east. Take a deep breath. Focus your intention on creating an energetic boundary to form your ritual space. Using the wand, athame, chalice, or index finger on your dominant hand, breathe deeply and visualize drawing up fiery or watery energy from the earth, through your body, and into the tool or your finger. If you haven't worked much with these types of energy before, fire energy will feel hot, powerful, and bright, whereas water energy will feel cool, flowing, and dark. As you exhale, visualize that energy pouring out of your fingertip or tool. Then move in a circle clockwise, starting and ending in the east, breathing energy up from the earth and out through your finger or tool, tracing that line of energy in a big circle around your ritual space.

DECLARE THE INTENT OF THE RITUAL

Say: "Today I will affirm and honor my sexuality, which I define as [word or words you use to describe your sexuality]. With the blessings of the Divine and the queer ancestors, I shall build an altar to my sexuality and toast myself."

WELCOME IN SPIRITS

Call to your chosen deity using their epithets. For example, say: "Aengus, young and fair god of love, son of the Dagda, I welcome you and ask you to join my rite this day. Please give your blessing to me and the altar I will create as I honor my sexuality. Hail and welcome."

Call to specific or general queer ancestors who share your sexual identity. Say: "[Word or words you use to describe your sexuality] ancestors, I invite you to join me in this rite, to lend me your power and guidance. Hail and welcome."

If you wish to welcome in any other deities, allies, and helper spirits, please do so in your own words.

RAISE ENERGY AND CONSCIOUSNESS

Take a deep breath and become aware of the water and fire within yourself. Focus on your heart, feeling the warmth and fluidity there and any emotions that come up as you consider your sexuality. Feel the heat of your blood, feel the pounding of your heart, feel the warmth of your desire. Breathe deeply. After a few breaths, direct your inner fire and water through your hand as you light the candle.

Close your eyes, breathe deeply again, and connect with the deities, spirits, and ancestors you invited to join your ritual. Talk to them about your sexuality, about what you've learned, and see if they have any wisdom to share with you.

DIRECT ENERGY, DECORATE THE ALTAR

Take a deep breath. Say: "I am [word or words you use to describe your sexuality]."

Begin to thoughtfully assemble your altar using the items you chose. Do this slowly, considering and carefully placing each item. It's okay to rearrange a bit as needed, and it's okay to leave a few things off if not everything fits the space. It's better to have it pulled together in a way that resonates and feels good than to include every single thing. Repeat "I am [word or words you use to describe your sexuality"] as often as it feels right to do so.

When the altar is assembled, take a moment to look at what you've created. What stands out to you? How do you feel when you look at the altar?

Toast Yourself

Take your wine or other beverage and your chocolate or other sweet treat and raise them up in the air. Ask the deity you called in to bless them. For example, say: "Aengus, I ask that you bless this [drink and treat], that they may nourish and enlighten me on my journey. I am proud to have figured out that I am [word or words you use to describe your sexuality], and though I know this is part of my journey and not a beginning or end unto itself, I celebrate this milestone."

Take a drink. Take a bite of the chocolate or other sweet treat. Relish the taste of them. If you wish, continue your conversation with your deities, spirits, and ancestors.

Thanks and Farewell

It is time to say your goodbyes to any spirits who attended the ritual. First, thank your chosen deity using their epithets. For example, say: "Aengus, god of love, I thank you for your blessing, guidance, and presence in my ritual here today. I bid you, go if you must, stay if you will. Hail and farewell."

Say farewell to the queer ancestors. Say: "[Word or words you use to describe your sexuality] ancestors, I thank you for your guidance and presence in my ritual. Hail and farewell."

Using your own words, say farewell to any other divine beings or helper spirits you called in to the ritual.

Close the Ritual

Blow out the candle.

Take a deep breath. Starting in the east, retrace your steps in a clockwise direction. As you do so, pull the energy from the circle of fire or water back into the tool or your finger, through your body, and back into the earth.

Post Ritual

Remember to ground and center yourself again, either with meditation or by eating or drinking something. Journal, draw, or record yourself speaking about your experience while it's fresh in your mind.

If you have any of the beverage leftover, you may pour it out somewhere outdoors as an offering of thanks to the divine being(s) and ancestors that assisted you in the ritual. Please do *not* leave anything chocolate outdoors, as it can harm dogs and other animals that may happen across it. I recommend consuming the entirety of the sweet treat, or if you must offer it up, do so in a protected area where no animals will get to it, in sacred fire, or in your garbage disposal.

You may keep the altar up as long as you wish, and relight the candle periodically as a reminder and reinforcement of the magick of the ritual. If you're unable or do not desire to keep the altar up, keep the components of it together in a box somewhere so you can rebuild it or repurpose items for future work. You may use the candle for other ritual purposes related to love and sexuality.

Name Change Ritual

Changing your name is both a huge step toward aligning your life with your affirmed gender and a fraught task logistically and emotionally. The process takes a ton of little steps, and the legal aspects can take months, if not years, to complete, depending on the name-change laws where you live.

Emotionally, changing your name can create pain and conflict with your family of origin, confusion among friends, and frustration for you. It would be nice to wave a magic wand and have the whole world immediately start using your correct name 100 percent of the time, but unfortunately, it takes a while before most people will use the new name consistently. All of this can erode your confidence in the name, and maybe even cause you to question whether the process is worth it.

Having gone through the process myself, I can assure you, it *is* worth it. There's definitely a euphoric feeling the first several months you hear people call you by a name that fits you better, one that resonates with who you are inside. It is worth celebrating, and worth recognizing in a ritual context.

This ritual will help your new name stick to you by making it resonate with all your parts of self. This is very similar to the ritual I performed when taking on my new name in 2020 and is adapted from a version of that ritual I published in *Queer Qabala*. Many thanks to Robin Fennelly, who contributed many components of this ritual.

Partners and Energies

The following partners and energies are particularly well-suited for this ritual's task.

Partners
- **Celtic:** The Morrigan (used as an example in this ritual), Rhiannon
- **Egyptian:** Ma'at, Hapi, Asushunamir, Atum
- **Greek:** Athena, Hermes, Hekate, Kybele
- **Norse:** Ođinn, Hervor, Freyja, Freyr, Loki

ANCESTORS

A call to queer ancestors is included in this rite. You may call whichever queer ancestors you wish, whether they are the stream of power of all the queer people who have existed before you, specific queer people from history, or queer people from your own lineage.

ENERGIES

* **Planet:** Mercury (aligns with the concepts of names and categories)
* **Qabala:** Hod
* **Element:** Earth (for the solidity of the change in the physical)
* **Tarot:** Knight of Pentacles

RECOMMENDED TIMING

Performing this ritual on any of the following days or at any of the following times will add power to this working.

* Your birthday, or the day immediately following
* **Day of the week:** Wednesday (for Mercury)
* **Planetary hour:** Mercury
* **Moon phase:** Full

RITUAL MATERIALS

* A marker, or a graphic design program and a printer
* A piece of cardstock
* A small table or altar
* An altar cloth of your choosing
* A pen
* A new, blank journal
* A taper or jar candle in a color that resonates with you and your new name (If you're undecided on color, use white or orange.)
* Lighter or matches
* *Optional:* eco-safe glitter and other craft supplies

SENSORY AND EMOTIONAL ENERGIES TO TIE IN

This is a ritual designed to bring you confidence in your new name. We will declare it with all parts of yourself and help it stick to you by integrating it more closely with your core self. Focus your thoughts and emotions on the certainty that this is your true name.

RITUAL PREPARATION

Spend some time thinking and writing about what your old name meant to you, why you were named that, and your feelings about releasing that name. (Do not use the journal you purchased for this ritual yet. Use a different journal, word processor, or a note-taking app.) If you were named after someone who is still living, depending on your relationship with them and how news of your name change has been received, it may be healing to have a conversation with that person, thanking them for the name and letting them know you are returning the name to them, perhaps to be passed on to someone new. If you were named after someone who has passed on, you may wish to write them a letter thanking them for the name and letting them know you're returning it to them so someone else can have it. You can then "send" your letter to them by either placing it on their grave, if you have access to it, or by carefully burning it in a heavy pot or other fireproof vessel and casting the ashes to the wind or into a body of water.

For this ritual, you will be charging a sigil to represent your new name and embedding it within multiple parts of yourself. A *sigil* is a magickal image composed of multiple connecting symbols arranged in a meaningful way. Before the ritual, spend some time creating a sigil with the letters of your new name. Play with rotating the letters, overlapping them, and connecting them in different ways until you have something that feels right. You can try incorporating other symbols that are meaningful to your transformation into the sigil, but don't overcomplicate it too much. Your name should be the focal point. Don't be hasty with this step—it will likely take a few tries before you create something you like.

Figure 1: Example Name Sigil for "Journey"

Draw or print the final sigil on the cardstock and cut around the edges of it. Add glitter or any crafty embellishments you wish.

Just before the time you plan to start your ritual, tidy up and then cleanse your working space with sacred smoke, a besom, or whatever space-clearing practice resonates with you. Put the altar cloth on the small table or altar. Place your sigil, pen, new journal, candle, and lighter or matches on the table or altar. Set up a chair if you don't want to sit on the floor for the meditation and journaling portions.

Ground and center yourself. Wash your hands with awareness of the sacredness of the water and all four elements present in the water, or use another purification method of your choosing.

THE RITUAL

You will now create your ritual container. Face east. Take a deep breath and let it out slowly. Inhale again, drawing warm, orange energy up from the earth into your body. As you exhale, push that energy out from the index finger on your dominant hand. Move clockwise around your ritual space, pushing the warm, orange energy out of your finger to trace an energetic line in a circle around your altar and where you will stand or sit during the ritual. Focus on creating a sharp boundary and container for your magick. If it is part of your practice, call to the elements in each quarter as you scribe the circle.

DECLARE THE INTENT OF THE RITUAL

Say: "On this day of [date], I honor my [old, birth, or previous] name, [old name]. I leave this name behind with love and gratitude for the ways it has served and supported me. I hold this name as the memory of who I was. In the beauty and truth of rebirth, growth, and transformation, I will claim the mantle of who I have become. In witness of the seen and unseen, I step into my power today by claiming a new name: [new name]."

WELCOME IN SPIRITS

Call to your chosen deity using their epithets. For example, say: "Hail Morrigan, goddess of sovereignty. I ask for your aid this day as I release my old name and embed a new name into all parts of myself. Please bless and protect my rite. Hail and welcome."

Call to the queer ancestors. Say: "Hail to all the queer ancestors, those who have blazed trails before me. I ask for your aid this day as I release my old name and embed a new name into all parts of myself. Please bless and protect my rite and guide me in the weeks ahead. Hail and welcome."

If you wish to welcome in any other deities, allies, and helper spirits, please do so in your own words.

RAISE CONSCIOUSNESS

Light your candle.

Hold up the new journal and say: "I dedicate this journal of naming that it may hold the words, wisdom, and vibration of who I am and how I am named in all of the worlds. May it know my names. May it know me."

Take up your sigil and say: "I call to the vibration and energetic signature of this, my name, [new name], that it may resonate and echo throughout all levels of my being in all of the worlds."

Awaken your lower self by focusing on your body's sensations and all your senses. Feel the surface you're standing or sitting on. Feel the clothes on your body. Note what you smell. Note what you hear. Focus your gaze on the sigil. Then say: "I awaken my lower self, the part of me focused on survival and immediate needs, that it may know me as [new name] in all of the worlds."

Awaken your middle self by focusing on your conscious mind and any thoughts floating around in it. Focus your gaze on the sigil again. Then say: "I awaken my middle self, the conscious part of me that makes decisions and moves through the world, that it may know me as [new name] in all of the worlds."

Awaken your higher self by humming or singing a high note and feeling the vibration through your whole body, then feeling that vibration expand outward, vibrating a tether that connects you to your eternal self in all times and places. Focus your gaze on the sigil once more. Then say: "I awaken my higher self, the part of me that is eternal, that it may know me as [new name] in all of the worlds."

Focus and Direct Energy

Open the journal. On the first page, write: *I am [new name].*

On the second page, write: *I am [new name].*

Below that, draw the Mercury symbol:

Figure 2: Mercury Symbol

Write below that: *By the naming and communication powers of Mercury, I declare this to be my true name.*

On the third page, write: *I am [new name].*

Below that, draw the Venus symbol:

Figure 3: Venus Symbol

Write below that: *With the love of Venus and love for myself, I declare this to be my true name.*

On the fourth page, write: *I am [new name].*
Below that, draw the Mars symbol:

Figure 4: Mars Symbol

Write below that: *With the courage of Mars, I declare this to be my true name.*
On the fifth page, write: *I am [new name].*
Below that, draw the Jupiter symbol:

Figure 5: Jupiter Symbol

Write below that: *With the visionary powers of Jupiter, I declare this to be my true name.*
On the sixth page, write: *I am [new name].*
Below that, draw a crescent moon:

Figure 6: Crescent Symbol

Write below that: *With the powers of the Moon, my unconscious mind, and the powers of my own birth and death, I declare this to be my true name.*
On the seventh page, write: *I am [new name].*

Below that, draw the Sun symbol:

Figure 7: Sun Symbol

Write below that: *With the bright, shining, healing powers of the Sun, I declare this to be my true name.*

On the eighth page, write: *I am [new name].*

Below that, draw a circle with an X in it to represent Earth and the material plane:

Figure 8: Earth Symbol

Write below that: *By the powers of Earth and manifestation on this plane, I declare this to be my true name.*

Spend some time meditating, communing with the deity, spirits, and ancestors you invited into the ritual, and seeing what messages come to you. When you are finished meditating, open your new journal and write any thoughts or observations starting on the ninth page.

Thanks and Farewell

It is time to say your goodbyes to any spirits who attended the ritual. First, thank your chosen deity using their epithets. For example, say: "Morrigan, goddess of sovereignty, I thank you for your aid, protection, and presence in this rite. I bid you hail and farewell."

Thank the queer ancestors. Say: "Queer ancestors, I thank you for blessing, protecting, and aiding my rite today. I bid you hail and farewell."

Using your own words, say farewell to any other divine beings or helper spirits you called in to the ritual.

Close the Ritual

Face east. Take a deep breath, and let it go. Using the index finger on your dominant hand, trace around the warm, orange energetic line you created at the beginning of the ritual, again moving clockwise around your space, starting and ending in the east. Focus on pulling that energetic line up through your finger, through your body, and back down into the earth. If it is part of your practice, thank and dismiss the elements in each quarter as you open the circle.

Post Ritual

Remember to ground and center yourself again, either with meditation or by eating or drinking something. Journal, draw, or record yourself speaking about your experience while it's fresh in your mind. If your legal-name-change process is still ongoing and you're able to do so, take one more concrete action toward finalizing it in the day following the ritual.

If it is safe to do so, leave your altar up with the candle lit for a few hours, or move the candle to another location to continue to burn for an hour or so. If you cannot keep it attended, leave it in a sink to minimize the risk of fire. Light the candle whenever you have feelings of uncertainty, impostor syndrome, or hardship around your name change. When it is fully burned down, dispose of what remains in a sacred fire if possible.

Keep the journal on your altar or in a special place. If you do future meditative or journey work around your new name, add notes from those experiences to your journal. Otherwise, keep it tucked away somewhere safe as a memento of this big change.

Pronoun Change Ritual

Changing pronouns can be exhilarating and euphoric, but also repetitive and exhausting. Especially at first, we are regularly misgendered and have to correct people over and over while they try to get the hang of our new pronouns. Early on, when I changed my pronouns to *they/them*, I only spoke up every fifth (or so) time someone used the wrong pronouns, because I simply didn't have the energy to correct people multiple times a day. It's scary, it's tedious, and sometimes it comes with a certain degree of self-imposed shame, particularly if we're older or come from a culture that places great value on *not being a bother* and *not standing out*. We're asking people to change their behavior for us. They need to rewire their brains a bit to accommodate an exception to rules they were taught at a very young age, rules that were ingrained over and over about which pronouns to use for which body features. We're throwing a wrench into something they thought they already understood.

There's also a certain amount of impostor syndrome that comes with this: people may wonder why you want to change pronouns, your gender, or both now, when you've seemingly been fine with the ones you've been using all your life.

This ritual aims to diminish that impostor syndrome, to affirm that your pronouns are yours, that they are part of you, and cannot be decided by others. By focusing on your sovereignty over yourself, saying a formal goodbye to your old pronouns, and *literally ingesting* your new pronouns, you will gain more confidence in using your new pronouns and correcting people who use the wrong ones, and help your new pronouns stick to you.

This ritual can be adapted for a group. Notes on how to do so can be found after the ritual.

PARTNERS AND ENERGIES

The following partners and energies are particularly well-suited for this ritual's task.

PARTNERS

- **Celtic:** The Morrigan, Brigid, Rhiannon
- **Egyptian:** Ma'at, Hapi, Asushunamir, Atum, Thoth
- **Greek:** Hermes (used as an example in this ritual), Kybele
- **Norse:** Hervor, Freyja, Freyr, Loki

ENERGIES

- **Planet:** Mercury (aligns with names and labels)
- **Qabala:** Hod
- **Element:** Earth (for the solidity of the change in the physical)
- **Tarot:** The Magician

RECOMMENDED TIMING

Performing this ritual on any of the following days or at any of the following times will add power to this working.

- **Day of the week:** Wednesday (for Mercury)
- **Planetary hour:** Mercury
- **Moon phase:** Full

RITUAL MATERIALS

- A black marker or pen
- 2 blank stickers, nametags, or labels
- A red marker or pen
- 2 firm sugar cookies
- Either a food-safe cookie-decorating marker or cake-decorating icing with a fine tip for piping writing
- Offering bowl or plate
- *Optional:* drum, rattle, or other percussion instrument; a jar candle

Note: This ritual calls for sugar cookies. If you can't obtain, bake, or eat this type of cookie, find some other kind of food you can write on that works with your dietary needs. Carving words with a butterknife or toothpick into something relatively soft works as well.

Sensory and Emotional Energies to Tie In

The emotional keys to this ritual are a sense of hope for the future and a sense of sovereignty over your life, body, and choices. As part of this ritual, you will be consuming a cookie, and you should savor the sweetness of that while also savoring the sweetness of aligning your labels to better fit who you are.

Ritual Preparation

Tidy up and then cleanse your working space with sacred smoke, a besom, or whatever space-clearing practice resonates with you. Set up your altar with the ritual materials. Set up a chair if you don't want to sit on the floor for the meditation portion.

Ground and center yourself. Wash your hands with awareness of the sacredness of the water and all four elements present in the water, or use another purification method of your choosing.

The Ritual

You will now create your ritual container. Take three deep breaths slowly. Breathe in through your nose and out through your mouth. Let your worries melt away, and feel yourself begin to focus on the magickal work that is about to take place.

Close your eyes. Visualize an orange sphere inside your chest, or feel a bubble of protective energy there, and feel it begin to slowly expand as you breathe. Whenever you breathe in, feel the power of that protective orange energy contract, and as you exhale, feel the sphere expand a bit further. Eventually, the sphere will surround you and then your working area. When you feel it is stable and adequately contains your working area, stop. Visualize or feel it holding in place, and feel its energy as a container for your ritual.

Declare the Intent of the Ritual

Say: "Until today, I have been using [old pronouns] as my pronouns. These pronouns have served their purpose, and, with love, I thank them for their service and let them go. Today, I take on new pronouns instead: [new pronouns]. I ask that the Divine and my helper spirits aid me in making this transition a joyful and satisfying one."

Welcome in Spirits

Call to your chosen deity using their epithets. For example, say: "Hail Hermes, wise counselor, who always has the right words. I call to you and ask for your aid this day as I change my pronouns from [old pronouns] to [new pronouns]. Please bless this transition, and guide my magick and my words today. Hail and welcome."

If you wish to welcome in any other deities, allies, and helper spirits, please do so in your own words.

Raise Energy

Stand or sit comfortably and focus on your breath for a moment.

Chant, with conviction, several times, until you feel enough energy has been raised:

I am me

I am free

I have sovereignty

If you have a drum, rattle, or other percussion instrument, play it while you chant.

Focus, Direct, and Release Energy

Using the black marker or pen, write your old pronouns on one nametag, sticker, or label. Stick it to your chest. Breathe in. Offer those pronouns gratitude for having served you in whatever way you feel is appropriate: out loud or energetically.

Remove the nametag and use the red pen or marker to cross out the old pronouns, focusing your intent on removing them from their association with you.

Say: "These pronouns no longer serve me. I bid them farewell."

Fold the sticker or nametag in half, tear it up into tiny pieces, and set them down or toss them in a nearby trash can.

Using the black marker or pen, write your new pronouns on the second nametag, sticker, or label, and stick it to your chest.

Say: "I declare, in this and all the worlds, that my pronouns are now [new pronouns]. May all I encounter address me as [new pronouns]."

Take the sugar cookies, and using either food-safe, edible marker or writing icing, write your new pronouns on both. Depending on your icing skill and space, you may shorten your pronouns to just one (e.g., "they" as opposed to "they/them/theirs").

Hold your hands over the cookies. Take a moment to breathe in, and imagine how sweet it will feel when somebody uses your pronouns correctly. As you breathe out, pour that happy energy into the cookies.

Hold the cookies up and ask your chosen deity to bless them. For example, say: "Hermes, I thank you for your aid this day. I ask for your blessing upon these cookies to empower me and make my new pronouns known to everyone in all the worlds."

Place one of the cookies on your offering bowl or plate and verbally offer it to your chosen deity. For example, say: "In gratitude, I offer you this cookie, great god Hermes. I give you thanks."

Eat the other cookie. As you chew and swallow, feel the strength and power of your new pronouns entering your body, connecting with your spirit, and sticking to your soul.

THANKS AND FAREWELL

It is time to say your goodbyes to any spirits who attended the ritual. First, thank your chosen deity using their epithets. For example, say: "Hermes, wise counselor, I give you thanks for your aid and presence in my ritual today. I bid you hail and farewell."

Using your own words, say farewell to any other divine beings or helper spirits you called in to the ritual.

CLOSE THE RITUAL

Return your attention to the orange, protective sphere you created. Visualize the sphere melting into the earth around you.

POST RITUAL

Remember to ground and center yourself again, either with meditation or by eating additional food or drinking something. Journal, draw, or record yourself speaking about your experience while it's fresh in your mind.

Offer the cookie for Hermes to the earth by placing it on the ground outdoors and saying, "I offer this cookie to Hermes." Do not put anything chocolate outside in a place where dogs or other animals may eat it, as it can make them ill. If you can't dispose of the cookie safely outside, eat it yourself or leave it on your altar, if you have one, for a couple of days before throwing it in the trash.

Throw the torn-up nametag in the trash if you haven't already done so. It's okay to throw away the other nametag after ritual too, but I recommend sticking it to a jar candle that you can light periodically to reinforce the magick of the ritual.

Within a day of the ritual, take actions to declare your pronouns to those you interact with: Tell people you're using these pronouns, gently correct people using your old pronouns, add your pronouns to your email signature and social media profiles, make or buy a pronoun pin, etc.

ADAPTATIONS FOR DOING THIS RITUAL AS A GROUP

You can do this ritual with the support of friends or other fellow magickal practitioners, whether everyone involved is changing pronouns or not.

Have everyone cast the circle together, with someone reading the instructions aloud. Tell people to see their orange spheres overlap and reinforce each other.

Change the "I" to "we" statements in the call to spirits, and adjust the wording to specify who is changing pronouns.

Leave the chant as is.

You will need more nametags and cookies to accommodate the number of people participating. If there are participants who are not changing pronouns, they may keep the first pronoun tag on their chest, and eat a cookie and offer a cookie with their current pronoun on it.

Replace the declaration with: "We declare, in this and all the worlds, that these are our pronouns. May all we encounter address us as such."

Replace the blessing with: "[Deity], we thank you for your aid this day. We ask for your blessing upon these cookies. Please empower us and make our pronouns known to everyone in all the worlds."

Change "I" statements to "we" in the thanks and farewell. Have somebody guide the group on visualizing the orange sphere you created together melt into the earth.

Ritual for Taking on a Drag or Gender-Bending Persona

Drag has a long history in the queer community, but has become riskier in the United States and other places in recent years. Many laws banning drag performances are being debated across the United States, and protests at drag events are becoming more common. Such laws are written and protests are held out of fear of cultural norms being challenged by drag, and are often used as a stepping stone toward further persecution of the queer community—in particular, transgender people.

Drag can be a powerful tool for exploring one's bodily sovereignty, experimenting with gender presentation and sexual expression, and just having fun with gender and sexuality.

This ritual helps you claim ownership of and empower a new drag or gender-bending persona. Before doing this ritual, you'll want to have your new persona fairly well-conceived, so if you haven't done so already, do some thinking, sketching, and journaling to figure out makeup looks, costumes, personality, humor, and other aspects of the character you want to portray. Choose a name and pull together at least one complete costume and makeup look to be worn during this ritual. When choosing the costume for this ritual, I encourage you to wear colors you feel are empowering. If you're not sure which colors are empowering for you, red is often a good choice. This ritual will then take the persona to the next level by helping to cultivate the relationship between your authentic self and the character you are developing. This will help you slip seamlessly into it when you want to and feel empowered by it when you need to. This ritual can also help overcome stage fright when you are in character as your persona. You're also going to be creating a piece of art featuring your persona's name as a reminder and magickal focus for when you transform yourself into that persona in the future.

This ritual should be conducted in a place where you can put on your costume and makeup, ideally someplace with good lighting. I recommend creating your ritual circle, in part, with eco-safe glitter, which you will vacuum or sweep up after ritual, but if this isn't practical for you, cast your circle using the method on page 32 of the Performing the Ritual chapter instead.

Note: I have used the pronouns "they/them/theirs" to refer to your persona in this ritual. Swap them out for your persona's correct pronouns. I've put the pronouns in brackets as a reminder to replace them if needed.

This ritual can be adapted for a group. Notes on how to do so can be found after the ritual.

PARTNERS AND ENERGIES

The following partners and energies are particularly well-suited for this ritual's task.

PARTNERS

+ **Celtic:** The Dagda, Cerridwen
+ **Egyptian:** Hapi, Asushunamir, and Atum
+ **Greek:** Dionysus (used as an example in this ritual), Kybele, the Muses
+ **Norse:** Oðinn, Thor, Loki

ANCESTORS

A call to drag performer ancestors is included in this rite. You may call to the stream of power of all drag performers throughout history, specific people from history, or people from your own lineage.

ENERGIES

+ **Planet:** Moon (for illusion)
+ **Qabala:** Yesod
+ **Element:** Water (for flexibility and fluidity)
+ **Tarot:** The Magician

Recommended Timing

Performing this ritual on any of the following days or at any of the following times will add power to this working.

- **Day of the week:** Monday (for Moon)
- **Planetary hour:** Moon
- **Moon phase:** Full

Ritual Materials

- A table and a mirror, a dresser with a mirror, or a table you can place near a wall-mounted mirror
- A playlist of music that makes you feel empowered and resonates with your persona, and headphones if necessary
- Perfume or cologne in a scent you feel your persona would like (If you can't tolerate strong scents, omit this.)
- Eco-safe glitter
- All the makeup needed for one look for your persona
- A complete costume for your persona
- A piece of cardstock
- Craft glue
- Markers or pens
- Other craft supplies you wish to incorporate
- Two portions of a sweet treat of some kind, e.g., chocolate
- An indulgent beverage (wine, hot chocolate, sweet liqueur, a mocktail or cocktail) and two glasses
- *Optional:* décor for the room suitable for your persona

Note: Remember when bringing music into ritual to download the music beforehand. Put your phone on airplane mode or close out any noisy programs on your computer so you aren't distracted by notifications during the ritual.

SENSORY AND EMOTIONAL ENERGIES TO TIE IN

This is a ritual about glamor, glitter, fashion, fame, courage, confidence, power, fun, and, above all, *joy*. As much as possible, make this a full-sensory ritual, incorporating luxurious textures, flavors, scents, tastes, and visuals. It should be a feast for all the senses!

RITUAL PREPARATION

Tidy up and then cleanse your working space with sacred smoke, a besom, or whatever space-clearing practice resonates with you. Set the ritual supplies on or near the table or dresser. Decorate the room if you wish.

Ground and center yourself. Wash your hands with awareness of the sacredness of the water and all four elements present in the water, or use another purification method of your choosing.

THE RITUAL

You will now create your ritual container. Press play on your playlist and put on your headphones if you're using them. Feel the music within you, and sing along if you like. Take note of the emotions the music stirs.

Take a deep breath. Focusing your intent on creating a place of luxury and sensuality, begin by spraying one spritz of perfume or cologne in each of the four cardinal directions, starting in the east and working clockwise to the north. (Omit this step if you can't tolerate strong scents.) Next, while focusing your intent on creating a protective, sparkly barrier around your ritual space, sprinkle eco-safe glitter, starting and ending in the east while moving clockwise in a circle big enough to contain your chair, the table or dresser, and your costume. Have fun with this! Move to the beat of the music!

DECLARE THE INTENT OF THE RITUAL

Pause the playlist.

Say: "Today I charge and empower my persona, [persona name], and connect [them] to myself."

WELCOME IN SPIRITS

Call to your chosen deity using their epithets. For example, say: "Hail Diony-sus, god of theater, gender-bending performer, reveler! You with the ever-present twinkle in your eye and flair for all things fabulous! I ask for your blessing and your presence as I charge and empower [persona name], that I may portray [them] confidently, [add other appropriate adverbs here, e.g., "entertainingly," "sen-sually," etc.]. Please guide me and celebrate with me! Hail and welcome!"

Call to the drag performer ancestors. Say: "Hail to my drag performer ances-tors, those who walked this path before me. I ask you to bring your fabulous, exu-berant energies into this ritual, to guide me and offer me your advice as I create my new persona of [persona name]. Hail and welcome!"

If you wish to welcome in any other deities, allies, and helper spirits, please do so in your own words.

RAISE ENERGY

Press play on the playlist. Spend some time enjoying the music and dancing around. As you focus on the music, imagine yourself as your persona on a stage, entertaining and receiving wild applause from the audience, or in whatever sce-nario is your dream for this persona.

FOCUS AND DIRECT ENERGY

Put on your makeup with intention. With each layer of makeup, see yourself adding layers of your persona over your authentic self. Have a conversation with Dionysus, the drag performer ancestors, or your preferred deity about the pro-cess. Talk, laugh, enjoy.

Put on your costume with intention. With each layer of clothing, see yourself adding the final layers of your persona over your authentic self. As you put on the last piece, feel that magick snap into place.

Take a moment to choose and shape your voice to match your persona. In this voice, say into the mirror while looking into your own eyes: "I am [persona name]."

Check yourself out in the mirror. Admire yourself. Feel confident. Feel your-self embodying your persona. If you have a routine or an act you're working on, practice it in front of the mirror. If not, have an in-character conversation with Dionysus, your preferred deity, or the drag performer ancestors about acts you might consider, and play with some ideas.

Now, create a sign with your persona's name using the cardstock, markers, pens, glue, and plenty of glitter. Write your persona's name large in the center, and decorate around it. You can add words that describe them or just decorate it however you please. Feel yourself embody your persona, but also feel your authentic self creating this as a sort of love letter to that persona. Feel the music move through you and into your artistic creation. Have fun!

If you so choose, you may dance around and sing for a while. Revel and enjoy what you've created!

When you're ready, celebrate by sharing your food and drink with the deities, ancestors, and spirits you've invited to the ritual. Pour a drink and set out a snack for them, and eat and drink your portions. Feel the joy and fun of your new persona, and share that joy with the spirits.

THANKS AND FAREWELL

Give thanks to the divine partners and energies that joined you. First, thank your chosen deity using their epithets. For example, say: "Dionysus, god of revelry! I thank you for your aid, guidance, and presence as I charged and empowered [persona name]. I bid you hail and farewell!"

Thank the drag performer ancestors. Say: "My dear ancestors of drag, my fabulous forerunners, I thank you for bringing your joy and energy to this ritual, and for your guidance as I charged and empowered [persona name]. I bid you hail and farewell!"

Using your own words, say farewell to any other divine beings or helper spirits you called in to the ritual.

CLOSE THE RITUAL

Closing this ritual is simple: let out a big cheer!

POST RITUAL

Put away your makeup and supplies, vacuum or sweep up the glitter and crumbs on the floor, and organize the space back to the way it was.

You may want to include the date and time of the ritual on the back or front of your artistic creation as a reminder of your persona's birthdate for future celebrations or for creating a natal chart for your persona.

Offer the spirits' portion of drink and food someplace outdoors if it's safe to do so. Please do *not* leave anything chocolate outdoors, as it can harm dogs or other animals that may happen across it. I recommend consuming the entirety of the sweet treat or leaving it on your altar, if you have one, for a couple of days before disposing of it in the trash.

Remember to ground and center yourself again, either with meditation or by eating or drinking something. Journal, draw, or record yourself speaking about your experience while it's fresh in your mind.

ADAPTATIONS FOR DOING THIS RITUAL WITH A GROUP

This ritual can easily be adapted to a group where everyone is at a similar stage of developing drag personas. Have everyone do all the steps together, and make sure there are plenty of mirrors and chairs so everyone can get ready at once. Change the "I" to "we" statements in the invitations and farewells to spirit. Enjoy in-character conversations, dance together, turn it into a party!

RITUAL FOR EMPOWERING
A SEX WORK PERSONA

If we claim to advocate for the queer community and those most marginalized within it, that includes sex workers. Many of the people who have fought and continue to fight for queer rights have been sex workers, including transgender Stonewall pioneers Marsha P. Johnson and Sylvia Rivera. Those who do sex work deserve respect, compassion, and protection from harm in their work and daily lives. Sex work is work, and sex workers are people.

Unfortunately, the queer community is often hostile toward sex workers, and sex work has become riskier in the United States and other places in recent years. Laws passed in the United States, in particular the Stop Enabling Sex Traffickers and Fight Online Sex Trafficking Acts (SESTA/FOSTA) have driven sex work further underground, endangering many sex workers, including many marginalized queer people. If you'd like to learn more, or better yet, take action to help reverse this trend, please see page 211 for a list of organizations that protect and advocate for sex workers.

This ritual is for sex workers to claim ownership of and empower a sex work persona, as well as invite in prosperity and protection from harm. This persona will empower your work and imbue you with confidence while helping you draw clear boundaries between your personal and professional lives and relationships. This ritual will also encourage you to practice self-care in this physically and emotionally demanding profession.

Before doing this ritual, you'll want to have a good sense of your sex work persona, including a name and clothing and makeup looks. This ritual will then strengthen the connection between your authentic self and the persona you are developing so you can slip seamlessly into your persona when you want to and feel empowered by it.

This ritual calls in queer sex worker ancestors. If you have any in particular you would like to connect with, please include them in the ritual. Marsha P. Johnson and Sylvia Rivera are good choices.

Note: I have used the pronouns "they/them/theirs" to refer to your persona in this ritual, but please swap them out for your persona's correct pronouns. I've put those pronouns in brackets as a reminder to replace them if needed.

This ritual can be adapted for a group. Notes on how to do so can be found after the ritual.

PARTNERS AND ENERGIES

The following partners and energies are particularly well-suited for this ritual's task.

PARTNERS

+ **Celtic:** Áine (used as an example in this ritual), the Morrigan, Rhiannon
+ **Egyptian:** Ma'at
+ **Greek:** Aphrodite, Dionysus
+ **Norse:** Freyja

ENERGIES

+ **Planet:** Moon (for mystery and illusion)
+ **Qabala:** Yesod
+ **Elements:** Water (for the fluidity of changing personas), earth (for prosperity), fire (for protection and empowerment)
+ **Tarot:** The Magician

RECOMMENDED TIMING

Performing this ritual on any of the following days or at any of the following times will add power to this working.

+ **Day of the week:** Monday (for Moon)
+ **Planetary hour:** Moon
+ **Moon phase:** Full

Ritual Materials

- A table and a mirror, a dresser with a mirror, or a table you can place near a wall-mounted mirror
- A playlist of music that makes you feel empowered, sexy, and resonates with your persona, and headphones if necessary
- All the makeup needed for one look for your persona
- A complete outfit for your persona
- Perfume or cologne in a scent that makes you feel strong, empowered, and sexy (If you can't tolerate strong scents, omit this.)
- A printed photo of yourself in your sex worker persona look or something close to it
- A black fine-tip paint pen
- A green paint pen
- A red paint pen

Note: In this ritual, you will need a photograph. If it isn't printed on glossy paper, regular markers can be used instead of paint pens. Just make sure they don't smear easily on the surface of the photo. Test a corner of the photo first if you're unsure.

Remember when bringing music into ritual to download the music beforehand. Put your phone on airplane mode or close out any noisy programs on your computer so you aren't distracted by notifications during the ritual.

Sensory and Emotional Energies to Tie In

This ritual is focused on empowering a version of yourself that is in control, prosperous, and protected from harm. Focus on your inner strength and resilience.

Ritual Preparation

Tidy up and then cleanse your working space with sacred smoke, a besom, or whatever space-clearing practice resonates with you.

Set the ritual supplies on or near the table or dresser. Set up a chair where you can sit and see the mirror.

Ground and center yourself. Wash your hands with awareness of the sacredness of the water and all four elements present in the water, or use another purification method of your choosing.

THE RITUAL

You will now create your ritual container. Face east. Close your eyes and take a few deep breaths. As you breathe, become conscious of the energy of the Moon above you. It may feel watery, fluid, mysterious, glimmering, and ephemeral. Inhale, drawing this energy into yourself. Then exhale, sending that energy out through the index finger of your dominant hand. Continue drawing the energy in on the inhale and sending the energy out through your finger on the exhale, and as you do, trace a circle of that Moon energy clockwise around the outside of your ritual space with your finger, ending where you began. Feel the Moon energy enclose and protect you in your space.

DECLARE THE INTENT OF THE RITUAL

Say: "Today I step into my persona as [persona name], connect [their] energy to myself, and empower and charge this persona with the energy of control, protection, and prosperity, that I may flourish, be healthy, have good boundaries, and be kept safe from harm in this work."

WELCOME IN SPIRITS

Call to your chosen deity using their epithets. For example, say: "Hail Áine, goddess of love and wealth! I ask for your blessing and your presence as I charge and empower my persona of [persona name], that I may prosper and be protected. Please guide me and protect me in this work. Hail and welcome!"

Call to the queer sex worker ancestors. Say: "I call to the queer sex worker ancestors, those who have traveled this path before me. Please bring me your wisdom and your protection as I empower and charge my new persona. Hail and welcome!"

If you wish to welcome in any other deities, allies, and helper spirits, please do so in your own words.

RAISE ENERGY AND CONSCIOUSNESS

Press play on your playlist and put on the headphones if you're using them. Feel the music within you, and sing along if you like. Take note of the emotions the music stirs.

Sit comfortably in front of the mirror and close your eyes. As you focus on the music, imagine yourself as your persona being financially successful, enjoying your work, getting compliments from clients, and flourishing. See yourself in that persona being physically and emotionally healthy, demonstrating good boundaries with clients, and being protected from harm. Focus on this image for a few minutes.

FOCUS AND DIRECT ENERGY

Put on your makeup with intention. With each layer of makeup, see yourself adding layers of your persona over your authentic self. Have a conversation with Áine, the queer sex worker ancestors, and your preferred deities or helper spirits about the process.

Put on your outfit with intention. With each layer of clothing, see yourself adding the final layers of your persona over your authentic self. As you put on the last piece, feel that magick snap into place.

Spray yourself with perfume or cologne. (Omit this step if you can't tolerate strong scents.)

Check yourself out in the mirror. Admire yourself. Feel confident. Feel empowered. Feel in control. Feel yourself embodying your persona.

Pause the music. In the voice of your persona, say into the mirror while looking into your own eyes: "I am [persona name]."

Take the printed photo of yourself. Using the black paint pen, write your persona name in the middle of the photo.

Close your eyes and breathe. Imagine yourself protected by your guides and helper spirits in your work, and working only with clients who respect you and will do you no harm. Open your eyes and use the black paint pen to draw a protection circle clockwise around yourself in the photo, a barrier protecting you from harm and repelling any potential clients with harmful intentions. Say: "May I be protected from harm in this work. May I be safely hidden from those who would do me harm in this work."

Close your eyes and breathe again. Imagine yourself setting a boundary between your personal heart and the heart you share with your clients. Open your eyes and use the red paint pen to draw a small heart over yourself in the photo. Then draw a clockwise circle around that heart, within the protection circle you already drew. Say: "May I set good boundaries between my personal heart and the heart I share with my clients."

Close your eyes and breathe once more. Imagine yourself taking good care of yourself with healthy habits and good self-care. Visualize yourself enforcing good boundaries with your time and energy, supporting you in your work. Open your eyes and use the green paint pen to draw a clockwise circle around you inside the black circle, a sort-of halo of health. Say: "May I remember the importance of caring for my body, heart, and mind in this work and practice good boundaries and good self-care."

Close your eyes and breathe one more time. Imagine yourself financially successful, having more than enough money to meet your needs and provide you comfort and stability. Focusing on that feeling, open your eyes and draw a green dollar sign or other currency symbol on the photo inside the protection and health circles. Say: "May this draw money and prosperity to me with harm to none."

Finally, hold your dominant hand over the photo. Breathe in deeply, drawing energy from the earth and sky into yourself. As you exhale, push that energy out through the palm of your dominant hand and into the photo. Feel the symbols you drew onto the photo come alive, and feel their energy sinking into the photo and into you as your persona.

Thanks and Farewell

It is time to say your goodbyes to any spirits who attended the ritual. First, thank your chosen deity using their epithets. For example, say: "Áine, goddess of love and wealth! I thank you for your aid and presence as I charged and empowered my persona, [persona name]. I ask you to continue to protect me and bring me prosperity in this work. I bid you hail and farewell!"

Thank the sex worker ancestors. Say: "Queer sex worker ancestors, I give you thanks for your guidance and protection in this ritual, and ask for your continued guidance and protection in my work. I bid you hail and farewell!"

Using your own words, say farewell to any other divine beings or helper spirits you called in to the ritual.

Close the Ritual

Face east. Close your eyes and take a few breaths. Become conscious of the glimmering, fluid energy of the Moon encircling your ritual space. Using the index finger on your dominant hand, inhale as you draw the Moon's energy back into you, and exhale to release it back into the earth while moving in a clockwise circle, starting and ending in the east.

Post Ritual

You may want to include the date and time of the ritual on the back of your photo for creating a natal chart for a new persona, or as a reminder to perform this ritual again annually on the same date to reinforce the magick.

Remember to ground and center yourself again, either with meditation or by eating or drinking something. Journal, draw, or record yourself speaking about your experience while it's fresh in your mind.

On full moons for as long as you feel it necessary, you may recharge the image and its protections. Hold your dominant hand over the photo. Breathe in deeply, drawing energy from the earth and sky into yourself. As you exhale, push that energy out through the palm of your dominant hand and into the photo. Feel the symbols you drew onto the photo come alive, and feel their energy again sinking into the photo and into you as your persona.

Adaptations for Doing This Ritual with a Group

This ritual can easily be adapted to a group of fellow sex workers. You may choose to do this ritual over video chat, in which case each person will need to cast the circle in their own space. If you are doing this ritual together in person, make sure there's enough room within the ritual circle for everyone to get dressed and enough mirrors for everyone to put on their makeup. Choose someone to cast the circle while others lend them energy. Whether in person or online, change the "I" to "we" statements in the invitations and farewells to spirits. Take turns declaring your personas. And consider toasting yourselves and your prosperous futures after the ritual with a glass of wine or other indulgent beverage!

Chapter 4
RITES FOR NEW EXPERIENCES

Once you've come to terms with your identity—a process you may experience several times in your life as new understandings emerge—you will likely experience a lot of *firsts*: Your first time telling someone your identity. Your first time taking hormones or getting a gender-affirming haircut. Your first relationship as a newly out queer person. Your first time visiting a queer space or event. Your first time advocating for queer causes. All of these firsts can be ritualized to bolster your courage as you take these bold steps into becoming your most authentic self and integrating yourself into the queer community.

Protection and Blessing Ritual for Someone About to Come Out

Coming out, the act of revealing your gender or sexuality to people, is an ongoing process throughout a queer person's life. It's not just a *one-and-done* event. Even if you've come out to your friends, coworkers, or family previously, you may end up changing jobs, moving somewhere new, or acquiring new family members through new relationships, so you may end up coming out many times in your life to a number of different people.

If you feel ready to come out, this ritual can help you gather the courage to do so, whether it's your first time or twentieth time. With the help of the deities or helper spirits you regularly work with, as well as the queer ancestors, you will gather strength into yourself and charge three crystals with courage, protection, and comfort to carry with you when you tell someone or a group of people your gender or sexuality for the first time.

Note: Coming out is a highly personal choice, and everyone's situation is different in terms of safety, security, and other personal considerations. Each individual is the best judge for when and if they should come out, so do not pressure others or yourself to do so.

This ritual can be adapted for a group. Notes on how to do so can be found after the ritual.

Partners and Energies

The following partners and energies are particularly well-suited for this ritual's task, as are any deities or spirits you work with regularly.

Partners
+ **Celtic:** Brigid, the Morrigan, Rhiannon
+ **Egyptian:** Hapi, Asushunamir, Atum

+ **Greek:** Athena, Ares, Kybele, Hermes
+ **Norse:** Freyja (used as an example in this ritual), Freyr

ANCESTORS

A call to queer ancestors is included in this rite. You may call whichever queer ancestors you wish, whether they are the stream of power of all the queer people who have existed before you, specific queer people from history, or queer people from your own lineage.

ENERGIES

+ **Planets:** Sun (for healing and truth), Mars (for courage and protection), Mercury (for communication)
+ **Qabala:** Tiphareth, Geburah, Hod
+ **Elements:** Water (for softness, gentleness, and comfort), fire (for courage and protection)
+ **Tarot:** Strength, the Sun

RECOMMENDED TIMING

Performing this ritual on any of the following days or at any of the following times will add power to this working.

+ **Days of the week:** Sunday (if working with the Sun), Tuesday (if working with Mars), or Wednesday (if working with Mercury)
+ **Planetary hours:** Sun, Mars, or Mercury
+ **Moon phases:** Waxing or full

RITUAL MATERIALS

+ 8 pieces of clear quartz, all approximately the same size (1 inch in diameter or larger)
+ A piece of bloodstone, about 1 inch in diameter
+ A piece of hematite, about 1 inch in diameter
+ A piece of aquamarine, about 1 inch in diameter
+ Sacred smoke, bells, or other materials to cleanse the stones
+ A small dish of water

- A soft sweater, sweatshirt, shawl, or wrap
- A small pouch to fit the hematite, bloodstone, and aquamarine

SENSORY AND EMOTIONAL ENERGIES TO TIE IN

This ritual should feel comforting and protecting while filling you with courage. Draw on the strength of your deities, helper spirits, guides, the queer ancestors, and your own inner strength, which may be hidden.

RITUAL PREPARATION

Crystals are wonderful energy sources, but they can also absorb unwanted energies around them and need regular cleansing. Prior to the ritual, cleanse the quartz, bloodstone, hematite, and aquamarine with sacred smoke, with bells, by leaving them in sunlight for a day, or with another method of your choosing. Do not use salt water, as it could corrode the hematite and aquamarine and could disintegrate the bloodstone.[17]

Tidy up and then cleanse your working space with sacred smoke, a besom, or whatever space-clearing practice resonates with you. Set up your altar with the ritual materials.

Ground and center yourself. Wash your hands with awareness of the sacredness of the water and all four elements present in the water, or use another purification method of your choosing.

THE RITUAL

You will now create your ritual container. Hold the quartz pieces in your dominant hand. Take a deep breath in, and as you exhale, send bright, clear energy into the stones. Visualize or imagine them glowing with bright light. Continue breathing in and exhaling, filling the stones with light until they feel warm and buzzy in

---

17. Ceida Uilyc, "How to Cleanse Hematite Crystals," AllCrystal, accessed February 24, 2024, https://www.allcrystal.com/articles/how-to-cleanse-hematite/; "Can Aquamarine Go in Water?" Moonlight Gems AZ, accessed February 24, 2024, https://www.moonlightgemsaz.com/can-aquamarine-go-in-water/; Ceida Uilyc, "24 Crystals That You Can and Can't Put in Salt," AllCrystal, accessed February 24, 2024, https://www.allcrystal.com/articles/list-of-crystals-that-can-go-in -salt/.

your hand. Arrange the stones evenly in a circle around your ritual space, starting in the east and moving clockwise around, placing one stone in each of the cardinal directions of east, south, west, and north, and the other four evenly between them. As you place each one, feel it connect to the one you placed before it. When they're all placed, go to the center of the circle and breathe deeply. As you breathe, reach out with your energy to the quartz, and feel the connection between each stone, and between the stones and yourself. Feel a protective barrier arise in the spaces between the stones, glowing warm and bright. Take one more deep breath and say: "I am protected."

DECLARE THE INTENT OF THE RITUAL

Say: "As I prepare to come out to [family, friends, colleagues, etc.], today I gather my courage and ask for the blessing and protection of [names of spirits and deities you wish to involve in the ritual], and the queer ancestors. Guide me and protect me through this important part of my journey to live an authentic life."

WELCOME IN SPIRITS

Call to your chosen deity using their epithets. For example, say: "Freyja, fierce warrior and goddess of love, I ask you to join me in this ritual and protect me as I take the big step of coming out as [gender/sexuality]."

Call to the queer ancestors. Say: "I call to those who have embarked on this journey before me, those queer ancestors who have boldly proclaimed their truth to family, friends, and colleagues. I also call to those who were unable to share their truth but wish they could have and support me in this endeavor. Please lend me your strength and protection in this rite, and in the days and weeks ahead. Hail and welcome!"

Call to any other spirits or helpers you wish to include in your own words.

RAISE CONSCIOUSNESS

Breathe deeply. Close your eyes. Have a conversation with your chosen deities and spirits and the queer ancestors. Ask them for advice, ask for their protection—whatever resonates with your needs for this rite.

When you've finished your conversation, feel and visualize yourself surrounded by your chosen deities and spirits and the queer ancestors. Feel and visualize yourself surrounded by the quartz circle. Feel protection and power surround you. Draw the circle of protection created by the crystals and the spirits closer in toward yourself until you can feel it as a protective bubble closely surrounding your physical body. Breathe more power into the protective bubble. If it feels right to do so, hum or sing additional energy into it.

FOCUS AND DIRECT ENERGY

Pick up the dish of water. Hold your dominant hand over it. Breathe. As you exhale, visualize glittery, happy energy filling the bowl and permeating the water. Say: "I bless this water with joy and with the knowledge that I am worthy as I am."

Pause to let those words sink in. Breathe. Then say: "I call blessings to myself."

Dip your fingers in the water and dab the water onto the middle of your forehead, your heart, and your belly. Breathe. Feel the blessing of the charged water.

Say: "I call courage to myself."

Hold the bloodstone in your dominant hand. Breathe deeply and feel your power deep within you. Feel yourself strong and resilient. If you have difficulty doing so, ask the spirits to lend support. Pour strong, resilient power through your hand into the bloodstone. Feel the stone holding that power. Feel its strength. Feel the courage and boldness it contains. Then set it down.

Say: "I call protection to myself."

Hold the hematite in your nondominant hand. Feel the stone's strength, coldness, and heaviness. Feel it as a form of armor, protecting you. Feel it gathering and neutralizing any of your anxieties or fears. Then set it down.

Say: "I call comfort to myself."

Hold the aquamarine in your dominant hand. Feel the stone's clarity and calmness. Feel it as a form of comfort. While keeping the stone in your hand, put on the sweater, sweatshirt, or wrap. Feel how cozy and comfortable it feels on your skin. Breathe. Send some of that comforting feeling into the aquamarine. Set down the stone.

THANKS AND FAREWELL

It is time to say your goodbyes to any spirits who attended the ritual. First, thank your chosen deity using their epithets. For example, say: "Freyja, fierce warrior and goddess of love, I give you thanks for your aid and protection in this ritual, and ask for your continued protection in the coming weeks. Hail and farewell."

Thank the queer ancestors: "Ancestors, I give you thanks for your strength and protection. I ask that you continue to be present with me and lend me your strength and protection as I come out to [my family/my friends/my coworkers]. Hail and farewell!"

Thank any other deities and spirits you invited into the ritual in your own words.

CLOSE THE RITUAL

Breathe deeply and visualize and feel the energy from the quartz circle seeping back into the earth. Gather the crystals to open the circle, starting in the east and moving clockwise around the circle.

POST RITUAL

Remember to ground and center yourself again, either with meditation or by eating or drinking something. Journal, draw, or record yourself speaking about your experience while it's fresh in your mind.

Put the bloodstone, hematite, and aquamarine in the pouch and keep it with you when you need courage, comfort, and protection. You could also consider making wire-wrapped jewelry with them so you can easily wear them instead of carrying them in your pocket. Any metal wire wrapping will work fine as long as your skin isn't sensitive to it. Cleanse the crystals monthly with sacred smoke, with bells, by leaving them in sunlight for a day, or with another method of your choosing. Remember not to use salt water. Redo the ritual parts focused on filling them with energy to recharge them as needed.

Keep the quartz crystals together in a pouch or bag to be reused for future protective rituals.

ADAPTATIONS FOR DOING THIS RITUAL WITH A GROUP

If you already have a group of people who are supportive of your gender and sexuality and you would like to do this ritual with them, it can be easily adapted for either an in-person or online ritual with the following changes.

If you're meeting in person, when casting the circle, you can have the other people direct their energy to the creation of the circle while one person places the crystals, or you could have different people place each piece of quartz in the circle. If you're meeting online, each person could contribute a piece of clear quartz and hold it during the casting, taking turns charging and connecting their crystal to the previous person's and forming an energetic circle inclusive of your various locations.

Whether you meet online or in person, when the intention of the ritual is declared, the focal person of the ritual reads it as written above, and all the others present (if in person) or a designated person (if online) may add: "Those of us gathered in solidarity with our beloved [brother/sister/sibling] are here to lend our power and strength to this rite, that [they] may have the strength and protection [they] need as [they] come out." Remember to replace the bracketed use of "they" with the person's correct pronouns if they use something different.

Individuals may be assigned to call in (and later bid farewell to) specific deities or spirits.

Individuals may call in (and later bid farewell to) specific queer ancestors to lend their power.

All may participate in seeking wisdom during the raising of consciousness and may share what they learn with each other.

The three stones can be held up by the focal person for all to see, that all present may send energy and charge them together. If meeting in person, after the stones are charged, if everyone is comfortable doing so (get consent ahead of time), a group hug would be appropriate.

If meeting in person, take down the circle in the same way you set it up, either with one person picking up the crystals and opening the circle, or with individuals picking up the crystal(s) they placed. Together, visualize the energy sinking into the earth. If online, each person holding a crystal can set it down and visualize its power sinking into the earth.

RITUAL FOR GENDER TRANSITION MILESTONES

The following ritual was written by Misha Magdalene. Misha is a queer, transgender witch and the author of one of my favorite books of all time, *Outside the Charmed Circle*. We connected in 2019 through a mutual friend who realized we were both creating queer magick–related content and have become nigh-inseparable since then.

Though I am a transgender nonbinary person, I have not had the medical transition experiences of many transgender people, and I wanted to include in this book the perspective of someone who has. Misha's magickal workings in *Outside the Charmed Circle* emphasize personal sovereignty in a profound way, and she was the perfect choice to create this beautiful ritual that can be used for a variety of gender transition experiences, from taking your first dose of hormones to getting your first gender-affirming haircut to preparing for gender-affirmation surgery.

◆ ◆ ◆

While there are no truly universal experiences shared by all transgender, nonbinary, gender-nonconforming, and gender-liminal people, one experience that can be truthfully called common among us is the desire to enact some kind of change in the way we present ourselves to the world. For some, these changes may be as seemingly mundane as changing the way they dress, using or eschewing cosmetics, or adopting a new way of cutting or styling their hair. For others, these changes may be as involved and life-changing as starting hormone replacement therapy (HRT) or going through gender-affirming surgeries, or as magical as adopting a new name by which they will be known.

It's not unreasonable to think of each of these as magical actions. After all, we are literally exerting our will to change the world both inside and outside ourselves. We are, in a very real sense, shapeshifting. However, this kind of shapeshifting is the opposite of a glamour to conceal the true self beneath an illusion of beauty. Quite the contrary, this shapeshifting is done to *reveal* the true self, long hidden beneath illusions of social expectation and cultural obligation.

This ritual is intended to affirm and support the shapeshifting work in which you are already engaged, or perhaps as a way to initiate the shapeshifting you intend to begin. It's repeatable any time you take some action to bring your body more closely into alignment with your gender, your spirit, your very self. As alluded to above, those actions may be everyday maintenance or once-in-a-lifetime experiences. This work is meant to support and sustain you in those acts, to reaffirm the purpose toward which you take those actions, and to remind you of your own bodily sovereignty.

PARTNERS AND ENERGIES

The following partners and energies are particularly well-suited for this ritual's task.

PARTNERS

- **Celtic:** Brigid, Cerridwen
- **Egyptian:** Hapi
- **Greek:** Hermes, Aphrodite, Hermaphroditus
- **Norse:** Freyja, Freyr, Loki

ANCESTORS

You may include queer ancestors in this rite. Call upon the stream of power of all queer ancestors, ancestors who share your type(s) of queerness, or specific queer ancestors from history or your lineage.

ENERGIES

- **Planets:** Moon (for imagination, flexibility, and change), Mercury (aligns with names, labels, categories, identities), Venus (aligns with the feeling of your gender)

+ **Qabala:** Yesod, Hod, Netzach
+ **Elements:** Earth (for changes in the physical realm), water (for flexibility and change)
+ **Tarot:** The Magician, the World

Recommended Timing

Performing this ritual on any of the following days or at any of the following times will add power to this working.

+ **Days of the week:** Monday (for Moon), Wednesday (for Mercury), or Friday (for Venus)
+ **Planetary hours:** Moon, Mercury, or Venus
+ **Moon phase:** Full

Ritual Materials

This ritual is meant to directly support and connect with physical actions related to your body identity and sovereignty. Have the necessary supplies ready for the thing you want to use this ritual for. Some examples may be cutting your hair, wearing a new outfit, taking a dose of hormones, preparing yourself for gender affirmation surgery, etc.

Ritual Preparation

Tidy up and then cleanse your working space with sacred smoke, a besom, or whatever space-clearing practice resonates with you. Set up your altar with the ritual materials. Set up a chair if you don't want to sit or lie on the floor.

Ground and center yourself. Wash your hands with awareness of the sacredness of the water and all four elements present in the water, or use another purification method of your choosing.

Sensory and Emotional Energies to Tie In

The emotional core of this ritual is joy, whether exuberant and defiant or simple and quiet: joy in your own autonomy and identity, and in the experience of claiming and living in your body as your authentic self. Perhaps more than any other, the sense of touch is intrinsically tied to this experience of joy in one's own selfhood and embodiment.

THE RITUAL

Assume a comfortable bodily pose, whatever that may mean for you: standing, sitting, lying down, or any other position in which you can rest, relax, and not be preoccupied with the maintenance of your body for a few minutes. Once you've settled into that pose and relaxed, pay attention to your breathing for just a moment. Begin to take slow, easy breaths, as deep as are comfortable without straining yourself. The goal is to get healthy oxygen into your body, not to prepare for deep-sea diving. Try to settle into a rhythm of breathing, but don't focus on it so hard that you stop relaxing. The point here is to get yourself into a space where you can exist as comfortably as possible in your body.

When you are ready, on an exhale, push a bright, happy bubble of protective energy out from your body to surround you. On each subsequent exhale, make the bubble larger until it encompasses the space where you will be performing the ritual.

DECLARE THE INTENT OF THE RITUAL

Say: "In this ritual, I claim myself."

WELCOME IN SPIRITS

If you wish to call upon the deities, powers, or spirits with whom you are allied, this would be an excellent time to do so by whatever means you find best. This is also an appropriate time to call in the trans and gender-liminal ancestors. I'm an informal sort of witch and sorceress, so I tend to simply call out to them with the words of my heart.

RAISE ENERGY AND CONSCIOUSNESS

As you continue to breathe slowly and evenly, begin by envisioning or imagining a bed of soft, pinkish-red embers banked in the depths of your belly, perhaps a handsbreadth below your navel. When you're ready, take a deep breath, hold it for just a moment, then blow out that breath into those glowing embers in your belly. Feel the air from your breathing fanning that glow brighter. Repeat this twice more, and on the third breath, see the embers flare into a blaze: warm, but pleasantly so. Feel that warmth filling your belly with its fiery rose-colored light, and from within its glow, say or think to yourself:

> **From the well of my body, I claim my Self,**
> **And none shall lay claim on who I know myself to be.**

Now, with that fire in your belly burning merrily, raise your attention to your own heart, and envision or imagine a pinpoint of white light, like a star in the night sky. Focus on that star, then blow another three deep breaths into that light, seeing its twinkling shine increase with each, until on the third it erupts into silver-white incandescence. Feel that luminescence shining within you, and from within its light, say or think to yourself:

> **From the well of my heart, I name my Self,**
> **And none shall have say over who I know myself to be.**

Finally, with the rose-colored fire and the white incandescence shining within you, raise your attention to your head, and envision or imagine a soft blue sparkling glow surrounding your mind like an iridescent azure halo. From the midst of that glow, blow another three deep breaths into the light, feeling the intensity increase with each breath, a whirling dance of brilliance in every shade of blue from near-white to deepest indigo, until on the third breath it flares into a solid arc of blue-white radiance. Feel the cool, clear aura surround you like the sweetest spring breeze, and from within its presence, say or think to yourself:

> **From the well of my mind, I proclaim my Self,**
> **And none shall hold sway over who I know myself to be.**

Take another three deep breaths, blowing your breath into each of the three wells, feeling each one respond to your breath and your focus. Now, take one final deep breath and see their light expand and intertwine with each other. Exhale slowly and see them forming a coruscating column of rainbow-tinged iridescence running the length of your body, from your belly through to your mind and back again. See this light and know it to be an image of your Self, of the truest and most authentic part of your being. Bask in the light of self-knowledge, then say or think:

> From the three wells of my being,
> I claim, name, and proclaim my Self.
> I am who I know myself to be,
> And I move from the core of my Self
> To bring myself into being.

Remain in silence and light for as long as you wish. When you are ready to act, take one more deep breath and blow it out with force into your own cupped hands, as if to catch the accumulated power you're exhaling. Feel that power within your hands—a tingle, a buzz, a warmth, a placid stillness—and know that this power is yours: raised through your body, directed by your will, glowing with the brilliance of your spirit.

FOCUS AND DIRECT ENERGY

Now, leave your relaxed pose and move your body around. Take the power you've raised and turn it toward the action you undertook this ritual to support. If your action has physical implements or materials (clothing, makeup, paperwork, medications, other tools or objects), handle those materials and *will* the power into them. If the action is focused more on your physical body, lay your hands on that part of your body and *will* the power into it. As you do so, remember that you are empowering your own shapeshifting, your own transformation to become who you are.

THANKS AND FAREWELL

Give thanks and bid farewell in the words of your heart to any beings you invited.

CLOSE THE RITUAL

Close your eyes and get comfortable once more. Visualize and feel the bright, happy bubble surrounding you, and on an exhale, see and feel it melt back into the earth.

The rite is ended. May you be blessed.

POST RITUAL

If you still have excess energy, ground it into the earth by touching the floor or the earth outside and letting the energy flow out of you. Move your body around: wiggle your fingers and toes, rub your arms, clap your hands—whatever you may need to do to reestablish your connection to your physical self. It's also a good idea to eat or drink something.

Remember to journal, draw, or record yourself speaking about your experience while it's fresh in your mind.

Ritual for Your First Visit to a Queer Space or Event

As you get comfortable with your queer identity, you'll likely want to engage, or engage more deeply, with your local queer community. Queer clubs, community centers, and events are great places to meet folks who are on a similar journey to yours, providing support and camaraderie as well as new friends and experiences. I've been friends for twenty-five years with people I met at my college's queer space!

Online groups are great and vital, but there is something especially potent—and particularly nerve-racking—about physically visiting a queer space or event. Even having been out as queer for as long as I have, my first time visiting my local weekly queer happy hour a year ago was scary, and I spent weeks psyching myself up for it! This ritual will help you get into a space of openness and bolster your courage for that first experience. By constructing a pride talisman that doubles as a quiet stim toy, you'll give yourself the strength and optimal frame of mind for meeting new people and having new experiences—and give yourself something to fidget with during the event if you need it. Fidgeting with the talisman will recharge it too!

It's always good to bring a trusted friend to your first queer community experience, if possible, for moral support and safety, and I encourage you to do this ritual together before you go to the event or space. This ritual can be a fun group activity—just make sure you have talisman materials for everyone. Further notes on how to adapt this ritual for a group can be found after the ritual.

Be mindful of fire safety when melting the ends of the cord. You only need to touch fire to the ends for a second or so, then quickly blow them out. Don't do this step near anything flammable.

PARTNERS AND ENERGIES

The following partners and energies are particularly well-suited for this ritual's task.

PARTNERS

+ **Celtic:** The Dagda
+ **Egyptian:** Bes (used as an example in this ritual), Ma'at
+ **Greek:** Dionysus, Hermes
+ **Norse:** Loki

ANCESTORS

A call to queer ancestors is included in this rite. You may call whichever queer ancestors you wish, whether they are the stream of power of all the queer people who have existed before you, specific queer people from history, or queer people from your own lineage.

ENERGIES

+ **Planet:** Sun (for openness and confidence)
+ **Qabala:** Tiphareth
+ **Element:** Water (for connection and community)
+ **Tarot:** The Sun, Three of Cups

RECOMMENDED TIMING

Performing this ritual on any of the following days or at any of the following times will add power to this working.

+ **Day of the week:** Sunday (for Sun)
+ **Planetary hour:** Sun
+ **Moon phase:** Waxing or full

RITUAL MATERIALS

+ 2 feet of 2 mm silk cord in a color of your choice (White or black, if you're unsure.)
+ Lighter or matches

- ✦ A drum or rattle
- ✦ 6 plastic pony beads, or other plastic or wooden beads with large holes, in pride flag colors of your choosing
- ✦ Sharp scissors
- ✦ A metal key ring

Note: When looking for beads for this ritual, make sure they have holes large enough to fit a key ring plus doubled-over silk cord. Test them out before beginning the ritual.

SENSORY AND EMOTIONAL ENERGIES TO TIE IN

In this ritual, you'll imbue your talisman with hope, openness, confidence, and courage. As you construct your talisman, it's important to focus on the feelings you want to carry into the queer space and event, as well as the feelings you hope and want the queer space or event to create within you.

RITUAL PREPARATION

Tidy up and then cleanse your working space with sacred smoke, a besom, or whatever space-clearing practice resonates with you. Set up your altar with the ritual materials.

Ground and center yourself. Wash your hands with awareness of the sacredness of the water and all four elements present in the water, or use another purification method of your choosing.

To make the cord easier to thread into the beads, melt the ends of the cord with the lighter or matches before the ritual.

THE RITUAL

You will now create your ritual container. Beat the drum or shake the rattle in a slow, steady rhythm while walking around the perimeter of your ritual space three times clockwise, starting and ending in the east. As you create the sound, focus your intent on the creation of a protective barrier or bubble containing your work. Each time you walk around the circle, the barrier gets stronger. Visualize the barrier in your mind. When you've completed your third walk around the space, shake the rattle or beat the drum rapidly with a flourish, then say: "The circle is cast. This space is protected."

DECLARE THE INTENT OF THE RITUAL

Say: "Today, I prepare myself for a new experience: my first time in a queer community space since coming out. Though I am apprehensive, I wish to approach this experience with openness and hope. In this ritual, I will make a talisman to both protect me and give me the courage to be myself in this space."

WELCOME IN SPIRITS

Call to your chosen deity using their epithets. For example, say: "Bes, protector, lover of merriment, I call to you and ask you to bless my ritual and aid me in the creation of a talisman for courage and openness to new experiences. Lend your joyful energy to my working, that I may approach this queer community experience with hope. Hail and welcome."

Call to the queer ancestors. Say: "Hail to all the queer ancestors, those who have blazed trails before me. I ask for your aid this day as I prepare for my first experience in a queer space since coming out. Please bless and protect my rite and be with me as I venture forth after this ritual. Hail and welcome."

If you wish to welcome in any other deities, allies, and helper spirits, please do so in your own words.

RAISE ENERGY

Beat the drum or shake the rattle in a slow, steady rhythm while saying the following in time with or in between the beats:

Courage, come to me

Pride, come to me

Ancestors, come to me

Open me to new experiences

Open me to meeting new people

Open me to connection

Open me to community

Bring me joy

Add additional desires if you like.

Visualize a bright, sparkling glow forming around you as you speak the words.

Repeat the list three times, seeing the sparkling glow grow stronger each time, ending by shaking the rattle or beating the drum rapidly.

Focus, Direct, and Release Energy

Pick up the beads and hold them in your dominant hand. Breathe deeply. Take a moment to visualize how you want your first queer community experience to go. How do you want to feel while you're there? How do you want to feel afterward? Picture yourself talking to people, making new friends, doing whatever activity is planned, and enjoying yourself. Breathe and concentrate. On a big exhale, push that image, that energy, those feelings into the beads.

Now lay out your beads in a line in the order you want them to appear on the talisman.

Take the first bead and thread the two ends of the cord across each other inside of it, pulling the bead to the center of the silk cord. Say: "I call courage into this bead."

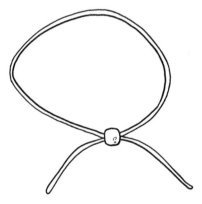

Figure 9: Thread the two ends of the cord through the first bead.

Figure 10: Pull the cord tightly.

Take the second bead and weave the two silk cord ends across each other through the bead, pulling it tight. Say: "I call pride into this bead."

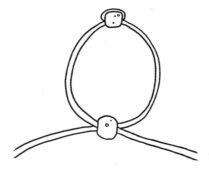

Figure 11: Thread the two ends of the cord through the second bead.

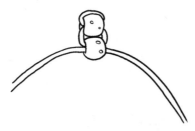

Figure 12: Pull the cord tightly.

As you string the third bead in the same way, say: "I call hope into this bead."

As you string the fourth bead in the same way, say: "I call openness to connection into this bead."

As you string the fifth bead in the same way, say: "I call joy into this bead."

As you string the sixth bead in the same way, say: "I call authenticity into this bead."

Tie the silk cord off in a secure knot, holding both ends together and tying a single knot with them at the base of the last bead. As you pull the knot tight, say: "This is my pride talisman."

Figure 13: Once you have all six beads threaded onto the cord, knot the end.

Trim the ends of the cord and melt them with the lighter or a match. Thread the key ring onto the first bead.

Figure 14: Trim and melt the ends of the cord.
Thread the keychain onto the first bead.

Hold the completed talisman up and say: "Whenever I am nervous or uncertain, I shall hold this talisman and fidget with it to feed it energy while drawing the emotions I spoke into the beads back into myself."

Drop your hand holding the talisman. Fidget with the beads a bit. Enjoy the smoothness of the cord and the beads.

Hold the talisman up again. Ask your chosen deity and the queer ancestors to bless the talisman. For example, say: "Bes, I ask you to add your power to this talisman, that I may approach this queer community experience with confidence and openness. Queer ancestors, I ask that you add your power to this talisman as well, that I may feel your strength and solidarity as I approach this new experience."

Feel the talisman radiate with power. Set it down on your altar.

THANKS AND FAREWELL

It is time to say your goodbyes to any spirits who attended the ritual. First, thank your chosen deity using their epithets. For example, say: "Bes, protector, lover of merriment, I thank you for lending your power, joy, and protection to this ritual and the creation of my talisman today. Hail and farewell."

To your queer ancestors, say: "Ancestors, I thank you for lending your strength and support to this ritual and the creation of my talisman today. Hail and farewell."

Using your own words, say farewell to any other divine beings or helper spirits you called in to the ritual.

CLOSE THE RITUAL

Beat the drum or shake the rattle rapidly, saying: "This rite is ended. I send this circle back into the earth."

Visualize the circle you cast earlier melting down into the earth.

POST RITUAL

Remember to ground and center yourself again, either with meditation or by eating or drinking something. Journal, draw, or record yourself speaking about your experience while it's fresh in your mind.

Bring your talisman with you to the event or community space, and fidget with it when you feel nervous or apprehensive. You may bring it with you to future events as well. When you feel you've gained what you need from it, cleanse your energy from it using one of the cleansing techniques on page 27. Recharge it by holding each individual bead and saying the powers you're imbuing it with, and tell the talisman you are gifting it to someone else in need, then pass it on to another newly out queer person.

ADAPTATIONS FOR DOING THIS RITUAL AS A GROUP

This is a fantastic ritual for a group. Even if others may have already attended a queer event or visited a queer space previously, everyone can use a confidence talisman and fidget toy. Make sure there are enough materials for everyone and adapt all the "I," "me," or "my" statements to "we," "us," or "our" statements in the ritual. Designate someone to play the drum or rattle and cast and dismiss the circle. Designate other people to welcome in and bid farewell to the deities, ancestors, and other spirits. Have another person read the statements aloud as call-and-response, or say them in unison.

RITUAL FOR ENTERING INTO YOUR FIRST QUEER RELATIONSHIP

The first time you enter a queer romantic or sexual relationship—any relationship where at least one of the people in it is openly queer—you may find yourself learning or relearning how to *be* in a romantic or sexual relationship. What feels authentic to you? What affirms your gender or sexuality? What affirms your partner's gender or sexuality? You may find yourself asking these questions even if you've been in the same relationship for years and stay in that relationship after one of you comes out. Coming out can make a relationship change in subtle, or sometimes drastic, ways. And even if you're in a relationship with a person who shares your newly discovered gender or sexuality, there may be situations where differences surface regarding comfort levels with various types of sexual acts, kink, or public displays of queerness. Or you may occasionally find yourself backsliding into previous, unhelpful patterns of behavior designed to push that person away emotionally. This may be because you don't want to admit you're scared to be living as your authentic gender or sexuality, or you're afraid to be seen and loved for who you really are. Stepping into your new identity can be equal parts amazing and terrifying, *particularly* when you start to feel affirmed. As writer Tim Kreider says, "If we want the rewards of being loved we have to submit to the mortifying ordeal of being known."[18]

Laying the groundwork early through a magickal working for a healthy, authentic partnership can really benefit your relationship in the long run. This ritual will help you set intentions for healthy communication, have the strength to be who you really are in the relationship and ask for what you need, and encourage you and your partner to see each other as you really are. Doing so may

---

18. Tim Kreider, "I Know What You Think of Me," *New York Times*, June 15, 2013, https://archive.nytimes.com/opinionator.blogs.nytimes.com/2013/06/15/i-know-what-you-think-of-me/.

reveal points of division or incompatibility, which you will need to deal with, but it can also bring you closer together faster.

PARTNERS AND ENERGIES

The following partners and energies are particularly well-suited for this ritual's task.

PARTNERS

+ **Celtic:** Áine, Flidais, the Morrigan, Rhiannon
+ **Egyptian:** Hathor, Ma'at
+ **Greek:** Aphrodite (used as an example in this ritual), Eros, Apollo, Artemis, Hermes
+ **Norse:** Freyja, Freyr

ENERGIES

+ **Planets:** Venus (for romantic love and sexuality) and Sun (for clarity and honesty)
+ **Qabala:** Netzach and Tiphareth
+ **Element:** Water (for relationships)
+ **Tarot:** Two of Cups

RECOMMENDED TIMING

Performing this ritual on any of the following days or at any of the following times will add power to this working.

+ **Days of the week:** Sunday (for Sun) or Friday (for Venus)
+ **Planetary hours:** Sun or Venus
+ **Moon phase:** Waxing

RITUAL MATERIALS

+ A piece of citrine, approximately 1–2 inches in diameter
+ Sacred smoke, bells, or other materials to cleanse the citrine
+ A journal and pen

- Small (2–3 inches wide) printout(s) of pride flag(s) that align with your gender and/or sexual identity (Or you can draw them if you don't have a printer.)
- A blank piece of paper
- Scissors
- A glue stick
- A red pen or marker
- A red rose (Or a different flower you associate with romance, if you're allergic to roses)
- A 7-inch-long piece of 1-inch-wide (or thinner) pretty ribbon

SENSORY AND EMOTIONAL ENERGIES TO TIE IN

Hope, resilience in the face of vulnerability, and determination are the best emotions to key into for this ritual. You must have hope for the future of the relationship, but also the willingness to be seen as the person you are and the determination to commit to yourself to be who you really are.

RITUAL PREPARATION

Citrine, like other crystals, can absorb unwanted energies around it and needs regular cleansing. Prior to the ritual, cleanse the citrine with sacred smoke, with bells, by leaving it in sunlight for a day, or with another method of your choosing. Tidy up and then cleanse your working space with sacred smoke, a besom, or whatever space-clearing practice resonates with you. Set up your altar with the ritual materials. Set up a chair if you don't want to sit on the floor for the meditation portion.

Ground and center yourself. Wash your hands with awareness of the sacredness of the water and all four elements present in the water, or use another purification method of your choosing.

THE RITUAL

You will now create your ritual container. Stand or sit in the middle of your ritual space and close your eyes. Take three deep breaths. Become aware of your heart beating. See and feel a warm, red ball of energy glowing in your heart center. As you exhale, expand that ball of energy, feeding it energy from your breath to push it wider and larger. Keep expanding it on every exhale until the ball is large enough to surround your ritual working space. Feel this ball of energy protecting you and serving as a barrier between your working space and the outside world.

DECLARE THE INTENT OF THE RITUAL

Say: "In this ritual today, I will lay the groundwork for a relationship in which I can be my authentic self. I am [describe your gender and sexuality in your own words]. I wish to be me and approach this relationship with honesty and integrity."

WELCOME IN SPIRITS

Call to your chosen deity using their epithets. For example, say: "Beautiful Aphrodite, goddess of love, romance, and sexuality, I ask you to join me in this ritual today as I lay the foundation for my first queer relationship. Bring me your wisdom and help me open my heart. Hail and welcome."

If you wish to welcome in any other deities, allies, and helper spirits, please do so in your own words.

RAISE CONSCIOUSNESS

Hold the citrine in your nondominant hand. Close your eyes and take a few deep breaths. Spend a few minutes focusing on the idea of you being your authentic self in a relationship. What will that look like? What will it feel like? How will different relationship milestones play out in that scenario? Imagine your partner, and imagine yourself interacting with them in a way that feels honest. See yourself speaking up for your needs. When you have a clear vision of the authentic relationship you desire, breathe into that idea and feel the energy from the citrine fill you with clarity.

Take a few moments to write in your journal:

- ✦ What actions will show that I am living out my intention to be fully myself in this relationship?
- ✦ What unhelpful old behaviors should I watch out for—ones that might indicate I am not living out my intention?
- ✦ What is a question I should ask myself each week to evaluate if I've stayed true to my intention?

Focus, Direct, and Release Energy

Cut a heart out of each pride flag you printed out. It may help to fold the paper in half down the middle of the pride flag to get the heart symmetrical.

As you use the glue stick to paste the hearts onto the middle of the blank piece of paper, focus on the aspect of your gender and sexual identity each flag represents and take a moment to send your heart some love and appreciation for these aspects of yourself, and for the courage it took to realize them.

Hold up the paper with the hearts glued to it. Say: "I am [describe your gender and sexual identity in your own words]. I will not hide [this or these part(s)] of me from my partner. I will be authentically myself, my whole self. I will clearly communicate who I am and what I need to my partner."

Add additional intentions as you see fit.

Seal those intentions into the paper by using the red pen or marker to draw a big red heart around the flag heart(s) pasted onto the paper. Being careful of thorns, wrap the paper loosely and gently around the stem of the rose, with the flag heart(s) facing outward, and tie it with the ribbon. Place it on your altar.

Focus on the wrapped rose for a moment, breathing deeply. See or feel your intentions radiating off the paper and the rose. Ask for the blessing and guidance of your chosen deity. For example, say: "Aphrodite, please bless my working today and my intentions. Guide me toward right action for me to be fully myself in this relationship. Thank you."

Remember what you wrote in your journal before. Dedicate yourself, in this moment, to routinely check in with yourself to ensure you are living out your intention. Say: "This is my Will. This is my commitment."

Thanks and Farewell

It is time to say your goodbyes to any spirits who attended the ritual. First, thank your chosen deity using their epithets. For example, say: "Beautiful Aphrodite, thank you for being present and for your blessing in this ritual. Hail and farewell."

Using your own words, say farewell to any other divine beings or helper spirits you called in to the ritual.

Close the Ritual

Sit in the center of your ritual space again. Breathe deeply and close your eyes. Feel the warm red bubble surrounding your space, and on each inhale, pull it back in toward your heart center.

Post Ritual

Remember to ground and center yourself again, either with meditation or by eating or drinking something. Journal, draw, or record yourself speaking about your experience while it's fresh in your mind.

Keep the rose on your altar until the petals become dry. Once they are dry, burn the rose and paper in sacred fire. You may choose to cut the rose and paper into smaller pieces so it will fit in a jar to save for the next time you have access to sacred fire.

RITUAL FOR ATTENDING YOUR FIRST POLITICAL ACTION

As queer people, our identities are politicized. Our very existence is controversial to some people. We are called to defend ourselves in public forums. Even if you've never considered yourself politically active before coming out, I hope you find yourself compelled to join the chorus of queer and ally voices speaking out to protect our human rights.

At one point in my career, I conducted grassroots advocacy trainings for people who had never been politically active before. I taught people how to call, write to, and visit their elected officials. And two of the main things I taught people are that you can make a big impact with small actions, and calling and visiting political leaders isn't as scary as it seems! (Pro tip: You can leave a voicemail for your elected officials after hours if you're scared to talk to someone in real time.)

Whether you're getting ready to attend your first protest or rally, speaking at a city council or school board meeting, testifying in a public hearing, or even simply calling an elected official, this ritual will help you pluck up your courage and rally your ancestral queer advocate allies by your side.

Political actions are less scary (and, in many cases, safer) when you do them as a group, and this ritual can be easily adapted for a group to perform together. See notes at the end of the ritual for guidance on how to do so.

If you're going to a protest or another event where you feel your safety may be at risk or there's a chance you may be arrested, please seek safety advice ahead of time from people who regularly participate in those kinds of events. You may need to leave your phone at home, wear an N95 mask, or take other preventative measures to protect your body and, in some cases, your identity. Be prepared.

PARTNERS AND ENERGIES

The following partners and energies are particularly well-suited for this ritual's task.

PARTNERS

- ✦ **Celtic:** The Morrigan, Rhiannon
- ✦ **Egyptian:** Sekhmet
- ✦ **Greek:** Athena (used as an example in this ritual), Themis
- ✦ **Norse:** Tyr

ANCESTORS

For this ritual, you'll connect with a queer ancestor who was active in advocacy. Ideally, find a queer person who was local to your region. If you don't know of any queer advocates from your region, do some research online or at your local public library: this is a great opportunity to broaden your queer ancestor pantheon. If you're stuck, consider researching and reaching out to the ancestral spirits of Audre Lorde, Harvey Milk, Marsha P. Johnson, or Sylvia Rivera.

ENERGIES

- ✦ **Planet:** Mars (for justice)
- ✦ **Qabala:** Geburah
- ✦ **Element:** Fire (for justice)
- ✦ **Tarot:** Justice

RECOMMENDED TIMING

It's best to perform this ritual right before when the political action is scheduled to take place, but performing this ritual on any of the following days or at any of the following times will add power to this working.

- ✦ **Day of the week:** Tuesday (for Mars)
- ✦ **Planetary hour:** Mars
- ✦ **Moon phase:** Full

Ritual Materials

+ A piece of hematite, approximately 1 inch in diameter
+ Materials for cleansing the hematite (e.g., incense, bells, etc.)
+ *Optional:*
  - Red candles
  - Mars sigil
  - Flag of the city, state, or country you are appealing to
  - Pride paraphernalia
  - Printout of text of legislative bill you will be advocating for or against
  - Photo of the queer ancestor you will be calling in to work with you

Note: For this ritual, you will create an altar that is focused on the concept of social justice. Some ideas for what to include are above. Add other items that resonate for you and the cause you're working for.

Sensory and Emotional Energies to Tie In

This ritual is designed to bolster your courage, and also to tap into your inner passion for justice. Feel the fires within you and see yourself ferocious and undaunted by fear: a proud warrior.

Ritual Preparation

Hematite can absorb unwanted energies around it and needs regular cleansing. Prior to the ritual, cleanse the hematite with sacred smoke, with bells, by leaving it in sunlight for a day, or with another method of your choosing. Do not use salt water, as it will corrode the hematite.[19]

Tidy up and then cleanse your working space with sacred smoke, a besom, or whatever space-clearing practice resonates with you. Set up your altar and decorate it with the social justice–focused materials you chose. Set up a chair if you don't want to sit on the floor for the meditation portion.

---

19. Ceida Uilyc, "How to Cleanse Hematite Crystals," AllCrystal, accessed February 24, 2024, https://www.allcrystal.com/articles/how-to-cleanse-hematite/.

Ground and center yourself. Wash your hands with awareness of the sacredness of the water and all four elements present in the water, or use another purification method of your choosing.

The Ritual

You will now create your ritual container. Sit or stand in the middle of your ritual space and close your eyes. Take three deep breaths. Become aware of your heart beating. See and feel a fiery, red ball of energy glowing in your heart center. As you exhale, expand that ball of energy, feeding it energy from your breath to push it wider and larger. Keep expanding it on every exhale until the ball is large enough to fit your ritual working space. Feel this fierce and strong ball of energy protecting you and serving as a barrier between your working space and the outside world.

Declare the Intent of the Ritual

Say: "As I prepare to [political action you are about to take], I find myself feeling [apprehensive/nervous/proud/righteous/etc.]. I seek to call on the spirit of [queer ancestor] to guide me, to grant me courage, and to keep me safe."

Welcome in Spirits

Call to your chosen deity using their epithets. For example, say: "Athena, wise protector, grant me your wisdom and your protection in this ritual, and as I [political action you are about to take]. Hail and welcome."

Call in the queer ancestor you have chosen to work with. Say: "I call to the spirit of the queer advocate [name]. [Say a few things you have learned about them in your research.] I seek your aid today as I prepare to [political action you are about to take]. Hail and welcome."

If you wish to welcome in any other deities, allies, and helper spirits, please do so in your own words.

Raise Consciousness

Sit comfortably. Take three deep, full breaths. Meditate for a moment while gazing at the altar you've created for this ritual.

Call to the queer ancestor. Say: "[Name], I ask for your guidance and your wisdom. What advice do you have for me as I prepare to [political action you are about to take]?"

Close your eyes and listen quietly to hear what the ancestor has to say to you. Open your eyes when you feel the conversation is complete.

Focus, Direct, and Release Energy

Hold up the piece of hematite. Say: "[Name of ancestor], I ask you to charge this hematite with courage. When I hold it, I will think of you and the courage you demonstrated when you [courageous action that person took]."

Keep holding up the hematite until it feels buzzy.

Thanks and Farewell

It is time to say your goodbyes to any spirits who attended the ritual. First, thank your chosen deity using their epithets. For example, say: "Athena, wise protector, I thank you for your presence and protection in my ritual today. Hail and farewell."

Then thank the ancestor you've invited to the ritual. Say: "[Name of ancestor], I am so grateful for your aid in this ritual. I ask that you stay with me as long as you are able as I [political action you are taking]. Hail and thank you."

Using your own words, say farewell to any other divine beings or helper spirits you called in to the ritual.

Close the Ritual

Sit or stand in the center of your ritual space again. Breathe deeply and close your eyes. Feel the fiery, red bubble surrounding your space, and on each inhale, pull it back in toward your heart center. Feel yourself become more courageous and fierce as you do so.

Post Ritual

Remember to ground and center yourself again, either with meditation or by eating or drinking something. Journal, draw, or record yourself speaking about your experience while it's fresh in your mind.

ADAPTATIONS FOR DOING THIS RITUAL AS A GROUP

This ritual is easily adapted to a group. Each person can contribute items to the altar. Make sure everyone has a piece of hematite and has researched a local queer advocate. Cast the circle together as someone talks everyone through how to create the fiery, red bubble. Feel your bubbles overlap and strengthen each other. Designate someone to call in and thank the deity, and then each individual should call in and thank their chosen queer ancestor and ask them for advice before you all sit with your eyes closed listening for their wisdom. Take turns holding up your piece of hematite and asking for your chosen ancestor to charge it. Visualize together the red protective bubbles being pulled back into your respective heart centers at the end.

Chapter 5
RITES FOR RELEASE AND HEALING

As you come to new understandings of your identity, sometimes old beliefs and parts of you need to be put to rest, and sometimes certain relationships become strained or unsafe to the point where they need to be released. There may also come a point where previously broken relationships can be reconciled. Using a ritual to release that which is no longer needed, and heal the past, can help you move forward into a more authentic, healthy life.

The rituals in this section can be done solo or with others. You may wish to involve others for support, especially since some of these rituals are emotionally heavy.

RITE TO BURY FALSE OATHS

The following ritual was written by Brandon Weston. Brandon is a nonbinary Ozark folk healer. I interviewed them as part of research for this book because I wanted to get perspectives from queer people from a variety of Pagan spiritual backgrounds, and in the course of that interview, I knew Brandon would be a phenomenal contributor. They were really inspired by the concept of a ritual to bury false oaths and crafted a beautiful ritual based on Ozark healing magick practices.

◆ ◆ ◆

Many of us grew up in communities where oath-taking was a vital part of religious and spiritual life. I took my own oaths as a kid: simple, but nonetheless binding. I remember the adults at my baptism said, "You can't go back." I didn't understand any of this at the time. When I was a teenager, I started hearing these threats more and more in my mind every time I had moments of gender dysphoria, or whenever I fell head over heels for a boy. "You can't go back," the voice would whisper to me. As an adult, I realized these oaths were false to begin with. Like a snake shedding its skin, I could now wiggle my way out from underneath the guilt. By burying those false oaths, I could be free.

These oaths can take on many different forms. Some oaths or promises you may wish to bury are ones you've made to yourself, in your own head, at some point in your life. Others may have been promises made to placate parents, friends, or others in less formal settings. Before you enter into the ritual space, examine what oaths you want to bury and write them down, however little they might seem.

This ritual is an amalgam of traditional Ozark cleansing practices and some of my own developments. This modern version of the practice is completely open to all magical practitioners, Ozark or otherwise. Feel free to take the parts that work for you and change or leave out the ones that don't. Your personal connection to the ritual is important.

Burying rites often feature as part of serious healing work in the Ozarks. In their simplest form, a person will be buried in a shallow grave (with their face above the dirt) overnight, then ritually exhumed at dawn and given a cleansing bath and new clothes. The idea is that whatever is cleansed off is left behind in the ground as the person is healed.

In my own modern reinterpretation of this work, we target the false oaths that were forced upon us as children, or any oaths made to yourself or others you wish to relinquish. We bind them to our own burial shroud. We sit vigil for ourselves, as solitary practitioners or with a trusted collaborator. We let the oaths die, remaining behind in the grave. We shed our old skin and emerge into the light of morning renewed and reborn.

You may do this ritual alone or have a partner to help guide the ritual. Adaptations for doing this with a partner are woven into the ritual.

PARTNERS AND ENERGIES

The following partners and energies are particularly well-suited for this ritual's task.

PARTNERS

+ Deities associated with death and dying (psychopomps especially) are great to include in this ritual.
+ **Celtic:** Ankou, Donn, the Cailleach, Annwn
+ **Egyptian:** Osiris
+ **Greek:** Persephone, Hekate
+ **Norse:** Hel

ENERGIES

+ **Planets:** Saturn (for boundaries and endings)
+ **Qabala:** Binah
+ **Element:** Water (for healing), earth (for burial)
+ **Tarot:** Death

Recommended Timing

Performing this ritual at midnight is strongly recommended. Other timings listed will add power to this working.

- **Time of Day:** Midnight
- **Day of the week:** Saturday (if working with Saturn)
- **Planetary hour:** Saturn
- **Moon phase:** Dark

Ritual Materials

You will need a set of materials to make a shroud, materials for a water bath, and other materials for the ritual itself.

For the Shroud
- A sheet big enough to fully wrap around your body, leaving just your head outside
- Food dye or natural pigments, any color
- A paintbrush in a size suitable for writing or painting words on the shroud
- A white cotton sheet or cotton broadcloth

Your sheet doesn't need to be new, so you might even be able to find an inexpensive white sheet at a thrift store or charity shop. Note that your final shroud will be buried at the end of the ritual, so I recommend using food dye or natural pigments that won't pollute the ground for writing on the sheet.

For the Ritual
- Black rope or yarn, long enough to make a full circle around your body while lying down
- A battery-powered light, any color or size
- Charcoal for loose incense
- An incense burner or heat-safe container
- Lighter or matches

- Incense options (can be combined): Red cedar leaves/berries (*Juniperus virginiana*) or common juniper leaves/berries (*Juniperus communis*), myrrh and/or frankincense resin, pine resin
- A blindfold or black handkerchief
- Scissors or knife

I recommend using a battery-powered light instead of a candle to decrease fire risk that could happen from wearing a shroud and trying to light and blow out a candle while sitting on the floor.

FOR THE WATER CLEANSING
- A large gallon pitcher, like that used for lemonade, or a similar pitcher or large bowl
- Water
- Salt, any kind
- *Optional:* herbs—any or a combination of hyssop, mint, sassafras leaves, juniper, or rosemary; mesh tea ball or small cloth bag for the herbs

FOR AFTER THE RITUAL
- A brand-new set of clothes
- A shovel (if burying your shroud), or a firepit or grill (if burning your shroud)
- Red cedar (*Juniperus virginiana*), or common juniper (*Juniperus communis*) incense

After an intense cleansing ritual and bath like this one, it's traditional to wear new clothes. This can be something simple and comfortable—even just a new T-shirt and pair of sweatpants. The key is the symbol of the new skin, so whatever items you choose, make sure they're brand new. For added resonance, Ozark healers will often ask their patient to wear a set of new white clothes, symbolic of cleansing and rebirth.

Sensory and Emotional Energies to Tie In

This ritual is a solemn one. You must go into it with reverence, the desire to rid yourself of your false oaths, and the strength to destroy them.

Ritual Preparation

This ritual has several preparation steps that take place over a few days and at specific times. Follow them carefully.

Making the Shroud

The shroud will symbolize the oaths to be buried.

Create your shroud in the days before the ritual burial. Take as much time as you need. Using the dye and paintbrush, write on the sheet all the oaths you want to release. Be as detailed as you can. You can also paint symbolic pictures if words can't capture what you are feeling. List out everything that has kept you in fetters.

Once everything is on the shroud, let it dry completely. At this point, you should also write down the last rites for the oaths you are burying, which will be read aloud during the burial ritual. This can be a story with an organized structure, a eulogy, or the words you painted onto the shroud. This is your process to connect to. The last rites are your opportunity to speak aloud the oaths you're cleansing and to make them manifest in the ritual space.

Setting the Space

I recommend a space where you will be secluded and free from distractions. A bedroom will work, as long as there is enough floor space for you to fully lay out on your back on the floor. If you have a physical limitation with lying on the floor, you may want to put some blankets or a foam pad underneath you, use your bed instead, or try other adaptations to accommodate. Discomfort is part of the experience; agony is not. Another *must* is that the space should be as dark as possible. This might mean hanging a blanket over windows, or making sure to stuff a towel across the bottom of your closed door. You may also need to cover LED lights on appliances and clocks.

Your room should be dimly lit for the first part of the ritual before becoming completely dark later. Place the battery-operated light within easy reach of the grave so you can turn it off later without leaving the grave or even sitting up.

PREPARING THE BATH

Before beginning the ritual, you will also want to prepare your water for the bath that ends the process. This is a simple Ozark method. Fill your plastic pitcher or large bowl with lukewarm water. Add three pinches of salt to the water as well as any herbs that you'd like to use. It's easiest if you add the herbs to a mesh tea ball or cloth bag so that you don't have to clean tiny bits of herbs from your tub, shower, or body later on. Leave the herbs in the water and place the pitcher on the floor of your shower or bathtub until you need it at the end of the ritual.

Set an alarm to wake you or alert you thirty minutes or so before sunrise.

MAKING THE GRAVE

On the evening of the ritual, make the symbolic grave. For this, you will use black rope or yarn. Knot the two ends of the yarn together to form a closed loop, then place it on the floor of your ritual space with the knotted end facing east. Next, stand or sit at the head of the grave (where the knot is) on the outside of the loop, facing the grave. Repeat this prayer: "My grave is dug. Under the black moon above me. My grave to hold me. My grave to cleanse me. Let what is buried here, remain here."

Fold the shroud and place it inside your symbolic grave.

When you're ready to begin the ritual, ground and center yourself. Wash your hands with awareness of the sacredness of the water and all four elements present in the water, or use another purification method of your choosing.

THE RITUAL

Traditionally, this ritual is performed at midnight—the liminal space between dusk and dawn. Begin outside your ritual room. Clothing is optional, but if you are going to wear something, make sure it's light and loose. Light your incense charcoal inside your holder. Add some of your incense. While holding your incense burner (on a heat-safe plate if needed) step into the ritual space and move in three counterclockwise circles around the outside of the grave. Let the incense continue to burn in a safe spot in the room, away from the grave and anything flammable. Adding additional incense to the coals is optional.

Next, stand or sit outside the grave at the head (where the knot is), so that you are facing west. Recite this invocation: "Whatever is buried is cleansed. I throw these oaths into the west! I throw them where all sickness and evil live! I seal them there until the stars fall from the sky. Holy Death, keeper of the grave, let me shed this old skin. Let me be reborn at dawn."

WELCOME IN SPIRITS

If you wish to welcome in any deities, allies, and helper spirits, please do so in your own words.

THE BURIAL

Make sure you have your written last rites with you, and get inside the grave. Face west (with the knot in the yarn or rope behind you). If you're working on your own, wrap the shroud semi-tightly around your shoulders, then lay down onto your back on the floor. The knot in the yarn or rope should be at your head. Adjust the shroud so that only your head is sticking out. If this is difficult, you can also lay down on your back, then spread the shroud over your body like a blanket. If you're working with a partner, have them wrap you in the shroud, then help lower you to the ground onto your back. Adjust the yarn circle around you if needed.

THE LAST RITES

Read the last rites to yourself, or have a partner read them aloud for you. Work at your own pace, taking pauses to visualize each oath as a monstrous form taking shape in the darkness around you. Know that while they might appear ferocious, they have no substance. They can't hurt you anymore. One by one, each oath falls into the grave, dead. Whatever form they might take decomposes and is reduced to bones, then to dust, then to dirt. Really feel this process happening. If it helps, you can also visualize the oaths getting sucked into the shroud around you, sealed there until their burial.

When you're finished, wrap the last rites pages in your shroud with you or have your partner do this for you. Extinguish the light. Put on your blindfold if you are working on your own, or have your partner put it on you. End the last rites in darkness and silence.

THE VIGIL

You can remain here for as long as you choose. Traditionally, the person being healed is left in the grave for the rest of the night until dawn. This is an option, but not necessary. If you plan to hold vigil until dawn, make sure your partner knows that they can also stay or leave the ritual space. They might want to sleep alongside you, in which case you should prepare bedding for them prior to the ritual beginning.

Sleeping in the ritual space can be powerful. You can even set up a pallet, sleeping bag, or makeshift bed inside the grave itself. Or you can sleep directly on the ground, allowing this uncomfortableness to add to the ritual itself. The grave is a grave, after all.

You can also choose to remain in the grave for a shorter meditation before sleeping through the rest of the night elsewhere. In this case, when you're ready, get out of the grave, move to your bed along with your shroud and grave rope. Surround yourself on the bed, or the whole bed if possible, with the black yarn or rope, with the knotted end at your head, forming a grave again. Cover yourself with the shroud while you sleep. You can use additional blankets as well, just make sure the shroud is on top.

The Exhumation at Dawn

When your alarm goes off, while it's still dark out, move out of the grave space (or your bed). Have your partner remove the shroud from around you, or you can remove it yourself. Fold for use later on.

Before you do anything else, even using the restroom, strip off your clothes (if you're wearing any), and stand or sit in your shower or bath. The pitcher or bowl of water, salt, and herbs that you made during the preparation stage should still be there. Face west, then say: "What is washed off is cleansed off. From my body to the grave."

Then pour some of the water over your head. Repeat the words, then pour some more of the water. Repeat the words a final time, and finish off the rest of the water in the pitcher. At this point, you can take a regular shower and make your other ablutions.

Your New Skin

Dress in your new clothes. I often recommend to my patients that they go outside and watch the sunrise if they're able. As you watch the sky go from black, to blue, to a myriad of colors, know that you are reborn as well. After doing so, finish waking up (which can include eating and drinking), then proceed to the final step of the ritual.

DESTROYING THE SHROUD

Traditionally, the shroud is left behind in the ground where the grave was dug. Since no physical grave was made as part of this specific ritual, you will need to take the shroud out and bury it somewhere. This can be a very intense moment, where the representation of oaths that had been such a visceral part of your body and spirit is finally laid to rest in the purifying earth. Find a spot that is relatively secluded and where you're safely able to dig a small hole. I don't recommend using your backyard, unless you have one that is large enough where there are places you can't easily see and don't regularly go to. This ritual aims to break free from these harmful oaths, and if you're constantly being reminded that they are buried around your home, you might not fully be able to let go. For this reason, I recommend taking the shroud out to the woods, desert, or other wilderness land. Check your local laws first, and be discreet and respectful.

Once you've located your spot, dig a hole large enough to accommodate the crumpled-up shroud. Take the shroud and place it in the ground. You can also add any other offerings or burial items you'd like, such as incense, flowers, food, drinks, etc. Cover the shroud with dirt so that none of it can be seen. At this point, you can read a final eulogy for your buried oaths, or simply return home without looking back.

If you're unable to bury your shroud, you can always cremate it. I recommend doing this outside in either a firepit or on a grill large enough to hold the shroud and any ash. Offerings and incense can also be thrown onto the fire during the cremation. Juniper is a traditional herb burned in the Ozarks during these burial rituals. Once the ash has completely cooled, take it and throw it into a graveyard or into a moving body of water like a creek or river.

THANKS AND FAREWELL

Using your own words, say farewell to any divine beings or helper spirits you called in to the ritual.

CLOSE THE RITUAL

You should cleanse the ritual space inside your home, especially if you used your own bedroom. Do this by circling the inside of the room three times in a counterclockwise direction with red cedar or juniper incense. Cleanse your bedding by washing it by hand or machine, making sure to add a pinch of salt to the water.

POST RITUAL

Remember to ground and center yourself again, either with meditation or by eating or drinking something. Journal, draw, or record yourself speaking about your experience while it's fresh in your mind.

INTEGRATION

The integration process for work like this is a slow one. Try as we might, there will always be things we've forgotten or overlooked. As you continue to grow, you might want to bury more oaths at another time, or even make this an annual event. Keep a journal of how you're feeling after the ritual. As more oaths rise to the surface, write them down. This ritual work reminds us that we are constantly growing and changing, just like the snake, who sheds its skin multiple times in its life.

Ensure you have support following this ritual. A trusted friend or mental health professional can help you process emotions that come up.

Funeral for Your Deadname

Even after you've affirmed your name and embedded it into all your parts of self, it takes a while for others to adapt to your new name. Getting repeatedly dead-named and misgendered takes an emotional toll, particularly if people are slow to correct themselves when they do so. While it's important to have compassion for yourself and others during this transition time, and to be patient while gently correcting people, there may come a point where you are just feeling very *done* and want to nudge the universe to speed things up already. If you've hit a point of frustration with repeatedly correcting people after several months, this ritual can help support mundane efforts to fully remove your deadname from your life.

In this ritual, you will lay your previous name to rest once and for all with a funeral rite wherein you will burn your old name written on a piece of paper. You will ask a psychopomp deity to take the name away from you and remove it from the lips of those who continue to use it.

This ritual can be adapted for a group. Notes on how to do so can be found after the ritual.

Partners and Energies

The following partners and energies are particularly well-suited for this ritual's task.

Partners

Psychopomps are particularly well-suited for this ritual.

- **Celtic:** The Morrigan
- **Egyptian:** Osiris, Anubis
- **Greek:** Hermes, Hekate
- **Norse:** Oðinn (used as an example in this ritual)

ENERGIES

+ **Planet:** Saturn (for endings and boundaries)
+ **Qabala:** Binah
+ **Element:** Fire (for cleansing, destroying, and transforming)
+ **Tarot:** Death

RECOMMENDED TIMING

Performing this ritual on any of the following days or at any of the following times will add power to this working.

+ **Day of the week:** Saturday (for Saturn)
+ **Planetary hour:** Saturn
+ **Moon phases:** Waning or dark

RITUAL MATERIALS

+ Paper
+ Pen
+ Lighter or matches
+ Firesafe container (iron cauldron, cooking pot, etc.)
+ A song appropriate for a funeral you can sing or play on your phone or computer, and headphones if necessary
+ An outfit appropriate to wear to a funeral

Note: Remember when bringing music into ritual to download the music beforehand. Put your phone on airplane mode or close out any noisy programs on your computer so you aren't distracted by notifications during the ritual.

SENSORY AND EMOTIONAL ENERGIES TO TIE IN

The most important feelings to call up within yourself during this ritual are confidence and assertiveness. Your old name is dead. You must hold certainty of this in your mind.

Ritual Preparation

In the days leading up to your ritual, write a eulogy for your deadname. Include how it has served you, but also how it is no longer your name. Write it in a way that feels authentic to you and your situation. Craft it carefully and thoughtfully. It doesn't need to sugarcoat your deadname or say a lot of flowery things about it unless you want to; the focus should be on how it is no longer your name, that it is dead and no longer yours. The eulogy does not need to be lengthy; a simple paragraph will do.

When you are ready to perform your ritual, tidy up and then cleanse your working space with sacred smoke, a besom, or whatever space-clearing practice resonates with you. Set up your altar with the ritual materials.

Put on the funeral outfit. Place all the ritual items on your altar.

Ground and center yourself. Wash your hands with awareness of the sacredness of the water and all four elements present in the water, or use another purification method of your choosing.

Write your deadname on the piece of paper. Embellish or decorate it if you wish.

The Ritual

You will now create your ritual container. Face east. Take a deep breath. Close your eyes and feel energy rising from the earth and down from the sky into you. Draw that energy into yourself as you inhale, and, using the index finger of your dominant hand, project a line of sharp, white energy in a circle as you exhale, moving clockwise around your ritual space as you do so, starting and ending in the east. When complete, feel the circle's power and protection.

Declare the Intent of the Ritual

Say: "Today I say goodbye to my deadname. Its time has passed, and in saying farewell, I will send it away from me and this material plane, so that those in my life may know me only by my one true name, [new name]."

Welcome in Spirits

Call to your chosen deity using their epithets. For example, say: "Hail, Odinn, psychopomp, you who takes the souls of the departed. Today I offer you my deadname, [deadname], and ask that you aid me in burying it and carrying it away from me. Hail and welcome!"

If you wish to welcome in any other deities, allies, and helper spirits, please do so in your own words.

Raise Energy

Play or sing the song you've chosen.

Read the eulogy out loud.

Take a few breaths and feel yourself ready to let your deadname go.

Focus and Release Energy

Hold the paper with your deadname on it over the fireproof container and carefully light it on fire, dropping it into the fireproof container once it's lit. Visualize the world forgetting your deadname and it being whisked away from you. (If you are in a space where open flames are not permitted, cut or tear the paper into tiny pieces instead.) As the paper finishes burning, imagine how it will feel when the world aligns to your new name and people call you your new name consistently and without struggle. Draw that joy and peace into yourself and breathe for a moment.

Say: "Odinn, I offer you these [ashes or pieces], all that remains of my deadname. Without causing them harm, I ask you to remove my deadname from the lips of those who continue to use it to refer to me."

Pause for a moment in gratitude.

Thanks and Farewell

It is time to say your goodbyes to any spirits who attended the ritual. First, thank your chosen deity using their epithets. For example, say: "Odinn, you who guides souls who have passed beyond this realm in death, I give you thanks for your guidance and assistance during this ritual today. Hail and farewell."

Using your own words, say farewell to any other divine beings or helper spirits you called in to the ritual.

CLOSE THE RITUAL

Face east. Take a deep breath. Close your eyes and feel the circle of bright white energy you created. As you inhale, draw that energy into yourself through the index finger of your dominant hand, then send it back down through you into the earth as you exhale, moving clockwise around your ritual space as you do so, starting and ending in the east.

POST RITUAL

Pour the ashes or torn-up pieces of paper down a drain or cast them in a moving body of water, like a river or stream, to be carried away. As you do so, say: "I commit these [ashes or pieces] to the underworld. Farewell."

Remember to ground and center yourself again, either with meditation or by eating or drinking something. Journal, draw, or record yourself speaking about your experience while it's fresh in your mind.

ADAPTATIONS FOR DOING THIS RITUAL WITH A GROUP

You can assign someone to cast the circle and another person to call in and bid farewell to spirits. You may ask others in the group to read their own eulogies for their own deadname(s). If the ritual is just for your own deadname, others may be willing to sing a song while you burn the paper. Most importantly, the people who participate can and should help emotionally support you after the ritual.

RITUAL TO SEVER TIES FROM UNSUPPORTIVE FAMILY AND FRIENDS

Many queer people experience the pain of having to cut ties from people, for safety and mental health reasons, after they come out. Some relatives or friends may react so poorly to someone coming out that a continued relationship will only be damaging for all parties involved, and a firm boundary and some physical and emotional space are necessary for healing.

If you are physically or severely emotionally threatened in your current situation, get yourself to safety before performing this ritual. Do not try to do this ritual if you are still living with people you need to sever ties with. This ritual is intended as a next step *after* you no longer live with them. What this ritual does is remove energetic connections between yourself and the person or people you need to sever ties with once you've gotten to safety. If you are not in a place where you can physically separate from the people who are causing you harm, instead of doing this ritual, I recommend focusing on setting emotional boundaries as much as possible to survive until you are in a place where you can physically separate. A trusted mental health professional can help you with this.

This ritual will sever energetic ties by physically cutting string connecting your names together and burning them, as well as burning down a black candle. Doing so will bring up painful emotions and memories. If you work with a therapist, talk to them about this ritual ahead of time and come up with a plan for how you will manage your care afterward. It may be good to schedule a therapy session a day or two after performing the ritual. Plan in advance for some self-care immediately after the ritual too: a treat to eat, a good talk with a close friend, some time spent outside, cuddles with a pet or comfort object, a good cry—whatever will help you process and transition back to your day-to-day life. I recommend letting someone you trust know ahead of time when you are doing this ritual, and asking them to check up on you shortly after it's complete.

This ritual can be adapted for a group. Notes on how to do so can be found after the ritual.

PARTNERS AND ENERGIES

The following partners and energies are particularly well-suited for this ritual's task.

PARTNERS

+ **Celtic:** Rhiannon, the Morrigan
+ **Egyptian:** Hapi
+ **Greek:** Hekate (used as an example in this ritual), Kybele
+ **Norse:** Fenrir

ANCESTORS

A call to queer ancestors is included in this rite. You may call whichever queer ancestors you wish, whether they are the stream of power of all the queer people who have existed before you, specific queer people from history, or queer people from your own lineage.

ENERGIES

+ **Planet:** Saturn (for boundaries and endings)
+ **Qabala:** Binah
+ **Elements:** Earth (for concrete changes in the physical realm) and fire (for destruction)
+ **Tarot:** Death

RECOMMENDED TIMING

Performing this ritual on any of the following days or at any of the following times will add power to this working.

+ **Day of the week:** Saturday (for Saturn)
+ **Planetary hour:** Saturn
+ **Moon phases:** Waning or dark

RITUAL MATERIALS

- Paper
- A pen
- About 1 foot of natural-fiber string, thread, or yarn per person you are severing ties with
- A pair of scissors
- A black chime candle and candleholder
- Lighter or matches
- A fireproof container (heavy pot or cauldron)
- A pair of metal tongs
- *Optional:* hole punch to make assembly easier

SENSORY AND EMOTIONAL ENERGIES TO TIE IN

The most important emotional energy to bring into this ritual is being certain of your conviction to remove this person or these people from your life. If you are hesitant, the ritual will be less effective, and it may be a sign you need to think on this decision further. You must be emotionally ready to fully cut ties before you enter into this ritual.

RITUAL PREPARATION

Cut out pieces of paper about 2 inches by 4 inches, and write the names of the people you are cutting ties with on them. Write your own name on an equal number of pieces of paper as the number of people you're cutting ties with.

Cut 1-foot lengths of string.

Punch a small hole in the end of each strip of paper with a pen, scissors, or hole punch, and gently, without ripping the paper, tie one end of a 6-inch piece of string to the name of a person you're cutting ties with. Tie the other end of the string to a slip of paper with your own name.

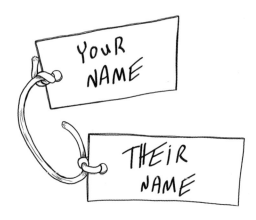

Figure 15: Piece of string with names tied to it

Tidy up and then cleanse your working space with sacred smoke, a besom, or whatever space-clearing practice resonates with you. Set up your altar with the ritual materials. Place the black candle in a candleholder inside the heavy pot or cauldron.

Ground and center yourself. Wash your hands with awareness of the sacredness of the water and all four elements present in the water, or use another purification method of your choosing. You may want to take a bath or shower with a salt scrub before or after this ritual to enhance the ritual's effectiveness at cutting ties. You can make your own salt scrub with a few tablespoons of kosher salt mixed with enough olive oil to form a paste, then scrub that paste all over yourself (be careful not to get any in your eyes or other sensitive areas) and rinse. Be sure to scrub the bottom of your tub or shower immediately after using it, as it can leave the floor quite slippery.

THE RITUAL

You will now create your ritual container. Face east. Take a deep breath. Focus your intention on creating an energetic boundary to form your ritual space. Breathe in deeply and visualize drawing up energy from the earth through your body. As you exhale, visualize that energy pouring out of the index finger of your dominant hand in the form of red fire. Then move in a circle, clockwise, starting and ending in the east, breathing energy up from the earth and out through your finger, tracing that line of red fire energy in a big circle around your ritual space. Focus on the fiery energetic line as a boundary, keeping in what is wanted and needed for the ritual, and keeping out that which isn't.

DECLARE THE INTENT OF THE RITUAL

Say: "Today I sever any and all energetic ties between myself and [name or names] for my own safety, protection, and emotional well-being. I did not arrive at this decision lightly, and I know it is the right path forward for me to flourish."

WELCOME IN SPIRITS

Call to your chosen deity using their epithets. For example, say: "Hekate, goddess of the crossroads, goddess of endings and beginnings, I ask for your strength and protection today as I cut ties between myself and [name or names]. Guide me toward successfully removing [this person or these people] from my life. Hail and welcome!"

You may also choose to invite in queer ancestors to assist in this rite. Say: "Hail to the beloved dead, those queer people who have blazed the trails I now walk. Please lend me your help and protection today as I cut ties between myself and [name or names]. Guide me toward successfully removing [this person or these people] from my life. Hail and welcome!"

If you wish to welcome in any other deities, allies, and helper spirits, please do so in your own words.

RAISE ENERGY

Light the candle inside the cauldron or heavy pot. Stare at the flame for a few breaths to clear and focus your mind.

When you're ready, hold one of the slips of paper with the name of a person you're removing from your life. Call to mind the relationship with that person. Think of moments you've had together and the pain that is driving you to remove them from your life. Pour that pain into the paper and string.

If you have additional pieces of string with names attached, repeat the meditation above with each.

FOCUS AND RELEASE ENERGY

Hold one of the pieces of string with names attached by the end with your name on it. Focus your intent on cutting this person out of your life, removing contact with them. When you are ready, take the scissors and cut the string so their name falls onto your altar or the floor (not in the cauldron or heavy pot yet). Repeat this process with each of the pieces of string with names attached.

Once they are all separated, take each of the severed pieces, including those with your own name, and, using the tongs, gently lower them into the cauldron so they catch the flame and burn to ash. As you do, imagine each relationship dissolving, all the energetic attachments being removed, all connections between you and that person being destroyed. Visualize tendrils of energy between you being cut and burned away. If any pieces fall into the cauldron without burning, use the tongs to fish them out and hold them to the flame again. Alternatively, if you're in a space where open flames aren't permitted, cut the paper and string into tiny pieces with the scissors.

Once complete, take a deep breath and close your eyes. Have a conversation with the spirit or deity you have brought into this ritual, and the queer ancestors if you invited them. Ask for their advice for next steps, for how to ensure this person or these people stay out of your life, and for how you can take steps toward healing and keeping safe from harm.

Finally, take some time to breathe in and draw some energy up from the earth to wrap around yourself as a comforting and protective barrier. Say: "May this shield protect me from those I have removed from my life. Their attempts to reconnect with me energetically, verbally, physically, electronically, or through others will fail."

THANKS AND FAREWELL

It is time to say your goodbyes to any spirits who attended the ritual. First, thank your chosen deity using their epithets. For example, say: "Hekate, goddess of the crossroads, I thank you for helping me navigate this crossroads in my life. I ask for your continued guidance and protection to keep [name or names] out of my life in the coming weeks. Hail and farewell."

If you invited in the queer ancestors, bid them farewell too. Say: "Beloved dead, queer ancestors who came before me, I thank you for your aid in this rite today. I ask for your continued help protecting me from [name or names] going forward. Hail and farewell."

Using your own words, say farewell to any other divine beings or helper spirits you called in to the ritual.

Close the Ritual

Take a deep breath. Using the index finger of your dominant hand, and starting in the east again, trace the same energetic circle around clockwise, but instead of sending the fire out of your finger, imagine it being pulled back into yourself through your finger on your inhales, and then down into the earth on your exhales.

Post Ritual

Let the candle burn down all the way. Do not leave the candle unattended, but if you must be away from it briefly, make sure it stays in the heatproof container or cauldron. It's okay if you can't burn it all in one go. When it's fully burned down, dispose of the candle stub and ashes in sacred fire if possible. Alternatively, take the candle stub and the ashes from the papers and string and leave them in a trash bin far away from your residence, school, workplace, or any other place you regularly visit. Toss them in, and walk away without looking back.

Remember to ground and center yourself again, either with meditation or by eating or drinking something. Journal, draw, or record yourself speaking about your experience while it's fresh in your mind.

Take some time for self-care after this ritual to process the emotions it has brought up.

Your mundane actions around this ritual are extremely important. If you haven't already done so, block the people you're severing ties with on social media, your phone, text, and email. Do not accept messages from them. Do not discuss them with other people, except to say you are not accepting contact from them and to process feelings confidentially with a mental health professional or trusted friend. Do not vent about them to everybody, and keep their name(s) out of your mouth as much as possible. Connect with one of the organizations for queer survivors of abuse if that fits your situation (page 208).

For a while, you may wish to revisualize the protective barrier once a day, then once a week, until it gets fully integrated into your aura.

Here are some ideas for additional work to call in healthy relationships to yourself: Journal about the qualities you'd like your future connections to have and why. Create and recite a daily mantra on how you deserve and welcome in healthy relationships. For example, say: "I deserve and welcome into my life healthy relationships that will aid in my growth while improving my mental and physical health." Write down a few key words of the types of things you're looking for in your relationships on a piece of paper, and keep it on your altar or in your wallet or pocket. Carry a piece of rose quartz with you.

ADAPTATIONS FOR DOING THIS RITUAL WITH A GROUP

Anyone joining this ritual can lend energetic support. You can assign someone to cast the circle, but you should be the one to call in and say farewell to the spirits gathered. While you meditate on and burn the names, the others present should focus on holding energetic space. You may wish to have someone softly drum or those present softly tone while you burn the names. When you pull the energy from the earth around you into a protective shield, that may be a wonderful moment for a group hug if everyone is comfortable doing so (get consent ahead of time). Everyone can lend their energy to your protection.

Most importantly, the people who participate can and should help emotionally support you after the ritual.

RITUAL TO RECONNECT WITH FAMILY AND FRIENDS

If you have severed ties with family or friends, there may come a time when you wish to reconcile and rebuild. This is not a decision to be made lightly. Make sure you are in a position of emotional strength and resiliency and are prepared to sever ties again if the person proves they can't be trusted and are still not safe to be around. Working with a mental health professional can be really helpful for assessing if you're in the right place for this.

This ritual is for opening your heart to give someone another chance, if you wish to do so. If you've previously disconnected from them energetically, this ritual will help reopen the lines of possibility for connection. It can also draw these people back into your life if you believe they've made amends or would be open to reconciling but you haven't been able to connect with them yet.

This ritual will invite reconnection through brief guided visualizations, then charging crystals for that purpose.

PARTNERS AND ENERGIES

The following partners and energies are particularly well-suited for this ritual's task.

PARTNERS
+ **Celtic:** Brigid (used as an example in this ritual)
+ **Egyptian:** Isis
+ **Greek:** Hera, Hestia
+ **Norse:** Odr, Aegir

ANCESTORS

A call to queer ancestors is included in this rite. You may call whichever queer ancestors you wish, whether they are the stream of power of all the queer people who have existed before you, specific queer people from history, or queer people from your own lineage.

ENERGIES
+ **Planet:** Sun (for healing)
+ **Qabala:** Tiphareth
+ **Element:** Water (for healing and connection)
+ **Tarot:** Two of Cups

RECOMMENDED TIMING

Performing this ritual on any of the following days or at any of the following times will add power to this working.

+ **Day of the week:** Sunday (for Sun)
+ **Planetary hour:** Sun
+ **Moon phase:** Waxing

RITUAL MATERIALS

+ Sacred smoke, bells, or other materials to cleanse the stones
+ A piece of rose quartz, about 1 inch in diameter
+ A piece of citrine, about 1 inch in diameter
+ A white tea light and holder
+ Lighter or matches

SENSORY AND EMOTIONAL ENERGIES TO TIE IN

This ritual is about healing, reconnection, and releasing past hurts. It is not necessarily about forgiving, unless that is your desire, but it does reflect a decision to move past the things that caused you to cut ties. Warmth and hope are key to help fuel this working.

RITUAL PREPARATION

Crystals are wonderful energy sources, but they can also absorb unwanted energies around them and need regular cleansing. Prior to the ritual, cleanse the rose quartz and citrine with sacred smoke, with bells, by leaving them in sunlight for a day, or with another method of your choosing. It is safe to use salt water to cleanse rose quartz and citrine, but don't leave the citrine in the water for very long, or it may damage the crystal. Rinse it off right away after dipping it in salt water.

Tidy up and then cleanse your working space with sacred smoke, a besom, or whatever space-clearing practice resonates with you. Set up your altar with the ritual materials.

Ground and center yourself. Wash your hands with awareness of the sacredness of the water and all four elements present in the water, or use another purification method of your choosing.

THE RITUAL

You will now create your ritual container. Face east. Take a deep breath. Focus your intention on creating an energetic boundary to form your ritual space. Breathe deeply and visualize drawing up cool, fluid water energy from the earth, through your body, and out through the index finger of your dominant hand. As you exhale, visualize that water energy pouring out of your fingertip. Then move clockwise around your space, starting and ending in the east, breathing water energy up from the earth and out through your finger, tracing that line of energy in a big circle around your ritual space. Focus on the energetic line as a boundary, keeping in what is wanted and needed for the ritual, and keeping out that which isn't.

DECLARE THE INTENT OF THE RITUAL

Say: "Today, I seek to open myself and set a beacon for reconciliation with [name or names]. I ask for divine guidance to ensure this is the right decision for me at this time."

WELCOME IN SPIRITS

Call to your chosen deity using their epithets. For example, say: "Brigid of the sacred healing well, I ask for your guidance and assistance as I open myself to mending my connection with [name or names]. Please lend me your wisdom and your healing touch. Hail and welcome!"

Call in the queer ancestors. Say: "I call to the mighty dead, those queer ancestors who have come before me. I ask for your strength, wisdom, and protection as I prepare to invite [name or names] back into my life, that this choice be for the good of all. Hail and welcome!"

If you wish to welcome in any other deities, allies, and helper spirits, please do so in your own words.

RAISE ENERGY AND CONSCIOUSNESS

Take a deep breath. Light the candle, envisioning it as a beacon, opening a pathway between you and the person or people you'd like to reconcile with. Take a few breaths, focusing on the flame.

Close your eyes. Call up your emotions around the person or people you're reaching out to. Remember both good times and bad, pleasure and pain. Remember the circumstances that caused you to part ways. Think on why you'd like to give the relationship another chance. Be honest with yourself. As you consider, the spirits or deities you included in the ritual and the queer ancestors may offer some advice. Listen.

FOCUS AND DIRECT ENERGY

When you are ready, open your eyes and hold the rose quartz in your nondominant hand. Place it over your heart and say: "I open myself to love and reconnection with [name or names]."

Breathe for a moment, feeling the energy between the stone and your heart. Visualize the stone growing until it is larger than your heart, surrounding your heart and protecting it with a loving glow. Set the rose quartz back on the altar.

Hold the citrine in your dominant hand. Place it over your heart and say: "I wish to take steps toward healing my relationship(s) with [name or names]."

Breathe for a moment, feeling the energy between the stone and your heart. Visualize the stone growing until it is larger than your heart, surrounding your heart and protecting it with a healing glow. Set the citrine back on the altar.

Finally, take a moment to visualize a road opening between you and the person or people you wish to reconnect with. That road should have lines or guardrails on it, denoting boundaries and where and how travel can happen, like a common paved street. Say: "I choose to make peace, but not at the expense of my inner peace."

Spend a few moments meditating on peace that does not come at the expense of your inner peace, on what the guardrails and boundaries with the relationship need to be if this person or people return to your life. Ask the spirits and ancestors you invited to the ritual for any final guidance they may offer.

THANKS AND FAREWELL

It is time to say your goodbyes to any spirits who attended the ritual. First, thank your chosen deity using their epithets. For example, say: "Brigid of the healing well, thank you for your guidance and healing touch in my ritual today. I ask for your continued guidance and protection as I explore reconciling with [name or names]. Hail and farewell."

Bid farewell to the queer ancestors. Say: "Queer ancestors, mighty dead, I thank you for your wisdom, strength, and protection in my ritual today. I ask for your continued guidance and protection as I explore reconciling with [name or names]. Hail and farewell."

Using your own words, say farewell to any other divine beings or helper spirits you called in to the ritual.

CLOSE THE RITUAL

Using the index finger of your dominant hand, and starting in the east again, trace the same circle around clockwise, but instead of sending the water energy out of your finger, imagine it being pulled back into yourself through your finger on your inhales, and then down into the earth on your exhales.

POST RITUAL

Remember to ground and center yourself again, either with meditation or by eating or drinking something. Journal, draw, or record yourself speaking about your experience while it's fresh in your mind.

Let the candle burn down all the way. Do not leave the candle unattended. It's okay if you can't burn it all in one go. When it's fully burned down, throw the candle stub in the trash.

You may wish to use the citrine and rose quartz as beacons and leave them on your altar, if you have one, or carry them with you in the days and weeks ahead, particularly if you might be seeing the person or people you wish to reconcile with.

As you reengage with this person or these people, have in mind a clear idea of your boundaries and what behaviors are unacceptable versus which are merely suboptimal. You should communicate to the person or people what behaviors will not be tolerated, and prepare to extend some grace for those behaviors that are not deal-breakers but are nonetheless disappointing while guiding that relationship to a more positive place. I encourage you to meditate, discern, and work with the deity or spirit who assisted you with this ritual and the queer ancestors to determine the best path forward for your health and well-being, and trust your gut.

Chapter 6
CELEBRATIONS

In this book, we've focused on exploring and affirming our own identities, new experiences, and release and healing. Most of the previous rituals in this book are designed to be done solo, with options for doing them with a group, in some cases. In this next section, however, all the rituals are designed to be done in groups. A very important piece of being queer is finding your people and feeling accepted within a community. Being seen in all your glory and having your identity witnessed and affirmed by others is incredibly powerful and can ease a lot of self-doubt and impostor syndrome. In these celebratory group rituals, you can be held and validated by others as you step into your authentic identity and form new relationships.

Chosen Family Hearth Ritual

The following ritual was written by Rev. Ron Padrón, who is a gay, disabled, Cuban American hedge priest and a dear friend of mine. His blog, whiterose witching.com, is a fantastic resource of queer, intersectional, magickal musings and practices, as well as wonderful profiles of a variety of queer ancestors. I was eager for an opportunity to collaborate with him, and as we tossed around possible ritual ideas, this one stuck out as something Ron was passionate about and that would be a useful and wonderful ritual to include in this book.

◆ ◆ ◆

For many members of the queer community, the idea of *family* can be challenging, traumatic, or even dangerous. Many are kicked out of their homes, endure physical or emotional abuse at the hands of relatives, or are forced to silo the LGBTQIAP2S+ part of their lives if they want to have any type of relationship with their families of origin. Even for those of us still in contact with our families, we can often feel isolated, as cisgender heterosexuals can never really understand our lived experience navigating a heterocisnormative society.

Many in the queer community end up finding or forming what is often referred to as a *chosen family*. This refers to a group of non-biologically related folks who provide ongoing support. These families become key to finding a sense of self and pride in one's identity, becoming resilient in the face of systemic oppression, and developing the types of connections we need in order to thrive.

The hearth has been considered the focal point of the home across time and cultures. It provides heat, is used to cook food, and oftentimes is incorporated into magical practice. It is common practice for the hearth to serve as a communal space for families to gather to share meals or just be in community. This ritual builds on the idea of the hearth as the physical and energetic anchor for a family, but expands it beyond the notions of the traditional family of origin and the constraints of a physical home. It brings together your chosen family through the creation of a symbolic hearth with the intention of imbuing a physical object with the protective, nurturing, and empowering energies we receive through those who care for us. For members of our chosen family who may not reside in the same home, the pieces of this hearth can be taken with them and placed in their own homes. By doing so, the spiritual hearth grows to encompass all residences associated with your chosen family.

The ritual outlined here is designed with the assumption that everyone who will be taking home a piece of the hearth is local, thereby allowing the use of larger stones or bricks. A suggestion for how to adapt this ritual to mail the blessed hearth pieces to nonlocal chosen family members is provided at the end.

PARTNERS AND ENERGIES
The following partners and energies are particularly well-suited for this ritual's task.

PARTNERS
* **Celtic:** Brigid
* **Egyptian:** Bastet
* **Greek:** Hestia
* **Norse:** Frigga

ANCESTORS
A call to queer ancestors is included in this rite. You may call whichever queer ancestors you wish, whether they are the stream of power of all the queer people who have existed before you, specific queer people from history, or queer people from your own lineage.

ENERGIES
* **Planet:** Sun (for healing and warmth)
* **Qabala:** Tiphareth
* **Elements:** Earth (for the physical hearth being built), water (for connections, emotions, relationships)
* **Tarot:** Ten of Cups, Four of Wands

RECOMMENDED TIMING

Performing this ritual on any of the following days or at any of the following times will add power to this working.

+ **Day of the week:** Sunday (if working with the Sun)
+ **Planetary hour:** Sun
+ **Moon phase:** Full

RITUAL MATERIALS

+ A brick for each individual
+ Sacred smoke, bells, or other materials to cleanse the bricks
+ An unscented candle for each individual, and candleholders if the candles are not freestanding
+ Lighter or matches
+ A bowl of salt water
+ *Optional:* cauldron

Note: In this ritual, you will be creating a hearth to contain the candles. Its size, which is determined by the number of people involved, determines the size and type of candle. If the overall size of the hearth ends up being relatively small (e.g., one square foot), you can use a cauldron to contain the candles instead of the hearth space. In that case, use white chime candles and holders.

If the hearth is large, candles of varying sizes and widths filling most of the central space will create a visually stunning centerpiece for the ritual.

SENSORY AND EMOTIONAL ENERGIES TO TIE IN

In this ritual, you and your chosen family will recognize your bond through celebration, joy, and reflecting on the moments you have supported each other. Moments of grief or sadness may be revisited in this ritual, but the focus is for participants to feel the warmth and safety that comes with the deep connections of your chosen family.

RITUAL PREPARATION

Conduct this ritual outdoors if possible. As it will involve fire, you should also make sure you have something to extinguish the fire readily available. Make sure the location where you will be conducting the ritual is thoroughly cleaned of anything combustible: dry leaves, twigs, etc., and that your space is reasonably shielded from the wind. If you must conduct the ritual indoors, make sure the space where the cauldron or candles will be placed is safely away from any draperies, blankets, papers, or anything else that could easily catch fire.

Set up the bricks in a large circle around the spot where you will be building the hearth. Each brick should correspond to where a participant will stand in the circle before placing their brick for the hearth.

If you have a large group, arrange the candles near the bricks, and keep the lighter or matches nearby. If you have a smaller group, put a number of candles equal to the number of participants in candleholders inside a cauldron.

It may be helpful for participants to discuss the shape of the hearth or arrangement of the bricks before the ritual. You can also let the energy of this ritual spontaneously guide you in how to build it if everyone is okay with that approach.

Energetically cleanse the bricks and candles or cauldron with sacred smoke, with bells, or with another method of your choosing.

Finally, make sure the bowl of salt water is nearby for participants to ground themselves when the ritual is complete.

The hearth has historically been a place where families gather for meals. It's a good idea to have snacks and drinks on hand for participants to enjoy, but I recommend participants attend to any biological needs before the ritual begins to prevent disruption.

This is a celebratory ritual. Participants should spend some time socializing and catching up before beginning. We want to bring in the joyous energy of being in community with those who support and sustain us.

THE RITUAL

To create the ritual container, gather in a circle around the area where you will build the hearth, with each person near a brick. Hold hands if it feels comfortable. Close your eyes and take three deep, calming breaths. Envision a circle of energy connecting each person in the circle, spreading down into the earth and arcing up into the sky.

Either one designated person or everyone gathered should say: "In our coming together we mark this circle as sacred. In our coming together we mark this place as hallowed ground. May no darkness enter, and only love abound."

Declare the Intent of the Ritual

Say together:

> We gather together in community as a chosen family.
> We are parents, siblings, children, and so much more.
> When one of us is cold, this family will warm them.
> When one of us is hungry, this family will feed them.
> When one of us is lost, this family is the light that guides them home.

Welcome in Spirits

Each participant should welcome in any divine beings and spirits they wish to include in the words of their heart.

One participant should welcome in the queer ancestors. If you wish to welcome in specific queer ancestors, add their names to the following. Say: "We welcome into this space our queer ancestors. We welcome those who traveled before us who, of necessity, came together and built their own families. From them we draw inspiration, strength, love, and courage. We honor their legacy; we cherish their memory. Hail and welcome."

Raise and Direct Energy

One at a time, each participant should pick up their brick and approach the center of the circle, placing their brick in the spot designated for the hearth, saying: "This chosen family is my home. From them I draw strength and stability."

Alternatively, you may choose to share a memory of when your chosen family provided you with strength or shelter.

Once all the bricks are placed, one at a time, each participant should take a candle, then place the candle on the hearth, making sure to leave at least a 6-inch perimeter around it. If you have a small number of participants, each participant should simply approach the cauldron containing the candles.

As each participant lights a candle, they should envision the flame as a beacon, drawing in the love they have for their chosen family. They should channel into that flame feelings of love, protection, and joy and envision those feelings traveling down the candle to suffuse the bricks. Once they have that feeling in focus, they should say: "This chosen family is my home. To them I give my love and protection."

Alternatively, each person may choose to share a memory of a time they felt loved and protected by their chosen family.

Once all participants have placed a brick and lit a candle, remain for a while in a circle. Hold hands if it feels comfortable. Allow participants to channel their feelings of love, protection, and joy into the completed hearth.

Depending on the size of the candles or fire, or how much time participants have to devote to the ritual, you may wish to let the candles burn down. If you choose to do this, it is fine for participants to wander, find somewhere comfortable to sit, eat and drink—but they should remain within sight of the hearth until the ritual is formally ended.

THANKS AND FAREWELL

One participant should say: "We stand in community not just with the living, but with the dead. As we here have chosen to support and care for one another, we know that our queer ancestors watch over us too. We thank you for the time spent together and bid you farewell."

If any divine beings or spirits were invited into the ritual, the participant who invited them should bid them farewell in the words of their heart.

CLOSE THE RITUAL

If the candles have not burned down, now is the time to extinguish them.

Come back together in a circle around the hearth. Hold hands if it feels comfortable.

Either one designated person or everyone gathered should say: "Though this ritual has ended, our hearth fire still burns. This hearth remains in spirit, as a place of gathering, a place of community, a place of safety, and a place of welcome."

Take three slow, deep breaths. Everyone visualize the circle cast at the beginning melting down into the earth.

POST RITUAL

Each participant should use the salt water to ground by washing their hands in it, splashing some on their face, or sprinkling some on the top of their head.

If participants do not live together, each participant should take a brick home with them to put on their altar, on their own hearth, or in a place that speaks to them.

Dispose of the remaining materials—candles, salt water—in whatever way is in alignment with your personal practice. You may choose to send each participant home with a candle to burn on top of their brick to recharge the energy as needed.

ADAPTATIONS FOR DOING THIS AS A REMOTE RITUAL

Your chosen family may be spread far and wide, so they may not be available to physically participate in this ritual. Below are some ways you can adapt this ritual to include folks virtually and in spirit. As in all things, consent is vitally important. Before conducting a version of the ritual where some will not be actively participating, be sure to get consent from those you want to include, and for you to act on their behalf. You may also want to arrange for them to send energy at the appointed ritual time in order to enhance the effect.

IF SOME MEMBERS ARE PHYSICALLY PRESENT AND SOME ARE NOT

You can include a spot within the area you will cast a circle to serve as a stand-in for members of your chosen family who are not physically present. Place however many bricks are necessary in that spot. Before beginning the ritual, decide who will serve as a stand-in for those not present. This might be a shared responsibility.

When it comes to the point in the ritual where you are laying bricks or placing and lighting candles, preface the appropriate statement with the following: "On behalf of [name], I declare:"

If you are able to have participants on video chat during the ritual, you can have each remote participant say their part as someone places the brick and lights the candle on their behalf.

Find a way to deliver the bricks to those who were not physically present. You may wish to use smaller stones to represent them so they're easier to mail.

FOR A RITUAL WHERE NO PARTICIPANTS ARE LOCAL

In this version you will be placing each stone on behalf of members of your chosen family with the intention of gifting them when your ritual is complete. I recommend substituting bricks for something smaller and easier to mail. You can purchase or find small river rocks, for example. Remember, get everyone's consent ahead of time before you do this ritual. If you're able, you can have everyone on a video chat while you do the ritual.

In place of building a hearth out of bricks, you can:

+ Use a tea light and ring it with the rocks.
+ Use a cauldron to contain a larger flame, and ring that with the river rocks too.

For this version, you should place the unlit tea light, or cauldron with an unlit candle in it, in front of you. The stack of rocks should be off to one side, with your grounding bowl of salt water on the other.

You can follow the steps in the group ritual above to create a ritual container, declare the intent of the ritual, and welcome in the spirits.

When it comes to the part of the ritual where you build the hearth, you will stack or arrange the rocks around your tea light or cauldron. If you are doing this ritual alone, you will state: "On behalf of [name], I declare: This chosen family is my home. From them I draw strength and stability."

Or if you're doing this ritual with people on video chat, each person will say the following as you place their stone: "This chosen family is my home. From them I draw strength and stability."

When it comes time to add fire to the hearth, light the tea light or cauldron and you (or each person on video chat, in unison) will state: "This chosen family is our home. To each and every one of us, we give our love and protection."

You can follow the instructions for thanking the spirits you called in, closing the ritual, and disposing of remaining ritual materials as outlined above. You now have smaller hearthstones you can gift to your chosen family.

Rite of Infinite Hearts: Handfasting Ritual for Two or More

The following ritual was written by Storm Faerywolf. Storm is a queer warlock and the author of *The Satyr's Kiss: Queer Men, Sex Magic & Modern Witchcraft*. I asked if he'd be willing to adapt the handfasting ritual from *The Satyr's Kiss* for this book, since it's a polyamorous-inclusive handfasting rite, and it was important to me to be polyamory-inclusive in this book. Though I am myself polyamorous, I have never performed a handfasting ritual, and I haven't had the opportunity to participate in a handfasting ritual for multiple people. Storm both has that experience and is a warm, kind human being and a fantastic writer. I'm honored to include him in this book.

✦ ✦ ✦

This is a ritual to formally bond two or more people together as committed life partners. It's both all-gender-inclusive and polyamory-inclusive.

Polyamory is a marginalized romantic identity. A polyamorous person has, or has a consistent desire to have, multiple romantic partners at once. Polyamory is built on the ideas of trust, honesty, and communication among all partners. Most countries' laws are not set up for multiple people to make legally binding, lifelong commitments to each other, but those with multiple partners who wish to publicly make those commitments to each other and celebrate their love can do so in a handfasting ceremony like this one.

This ritual involves a special rope or cord being draped over the clasped hands of those being joined. A blessing is usually spoken while the cord is partially tied, and then the couple or group carefully removes their hands from the cord, which is then tied into a knot. The knotted cords are then saved as a talisman for love, prosperity, health, and protection of the marriage.

Though this ritual uses the term *officiant* in the singular, multiple officiants may perform this ritual together if so desired.

PARTNERS AND ENERGIES

The following partners and energies are particularly well-suited for this ritual's task.

PARTNERS

While deities of love and marriage are obvious choices, this is incredibly personal and will be dependent on the practices of those involved. I recommend that if the partners each wish to have certain deities or spirits invoked, they should maintain a practice of invoking them together for an extended period beforehand as a means to magically prepare.

- ✦ **Celtic:** Aengus
- ✦ **Greek:** Aphrodite, Anteros
- ✦ **Egyptian:** Hathor, Bes
- ✦ **Norse:** Freyja

ENERGIES

- ✦ **Planets:** Sun (for healing and warmth), Venus (for love)
- ✦ **Qabala:** Tiphareth, Netzach
- ✦ **Element:** Water (for connections, emotions, relationships)
- ✦ **Tarot:** Three of Cups, Ten of Cups, Four of Wands

RECOMMENDED TIMING

Performing this ritual on any of the following days or at any of the following times will add power to this working. More personalized magical timing might be deduced from consulting the astrological charts of those being joined and looking for how the Moon signs of the partners interact.

- ✦ **Days of the week:** Sunday (if working with the Sun), Friday (if working with Venus)
- ✦ **Planetary hours:** Sun, Venus
- ✦ **Moon phase:** Full or waxing

Ritual Materials

- A strand of uniquely colored ribbon or silk cord for each person being joined (These should all be the same width, length, and thickness.)
- A large white pillar candle
- Lighter or matches
- A bell
- Some incense and a burner or holder, and charcoal if it's loose incense
- A red candle of any size, preferably the same size or smaller than the white pillar
- A chalice or bowl of water
- A stone or bowl of fresh soil, preferably from the local land
- An item from each handfastee that symbolically represents their old life, which will now be shed, such as an article of clothing, a piece of jewelry, or even a created object like a mojo bag
- Sacred smoke, bells, salt water, or other materials for ritual cleansing of those being joined
- A white taper for each person being joined
- A candleholder and bobeche to catch the wax drips for each of the white tapers
- A large cauldron or firepit, or black cloth
- A chalice for each person being joined
- Wine, champagne, juice, or other celebratory beverage

Note: Always practice fire safety and know where the nearest fire extinguisher is. If you wish to have a fire in your cauldron, you should prepare it beforehand with whatever you normally use to light a fire within it. Or you may wish to have a "symbolic fire" by using the cauldron to house burning white taper candles.

If you do not have a firepit and your cauldron is too small to burn the symbolic objects, you will also wish to have a large, black cloth placed open on the ground beside the cauldron on which these objects will be placed.

The items from each handfastee will be destroyed or buried as part of the ritual. If you will be burying items, be sure they are biodegradable.

HOW TO TIE THE INFINITY KNOT

As part of the handfasting, the officiant will tie an infinity knot around the hands of those being joined. These instructions and illustrations are based on those given by Jessica Levey for American Marriage Ministries.[20] They show the process using a single cord. The process is the same for using multiple cords. There are many videos on the web that demonstrate how to do this. Be sure to practice tying this knot beforehand. Tying this knot is actually very easy once you know how. Just practice a couple times and you will be sure to get it right.

1. Obtain your cord(s). They should all be the same width, thickness, and length.

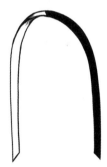

Figure 16: Infinity knot step 1

2. Those being joined should be facing each other and join hands in between them.

Figure 17: Infinity knot step 2

---

20. Jessica Levey, "How to Tie a Handfasting Cord—The Infinity Knot," *American Weddings Blog* (blog), American Marriage Ministries, updated December 2023, https://theamm .org/articles/595-how-to-tie-a-handfasting-cord-the-infinity-knot.

3. Drape the cords over the hands of those being joined so that the ends hang down of equal distance on both sides.

Figure 18: Infinity knot step 3

4. The officiant uses their right hand to firmly take hold of the front cord(s). They will not let go, keeping the cord stationary until the knot is complete.
5. The officiant takes their left hand and grasps the cords in the back, bringing them forward and under the hands.
6. The officiant brings the cord in the back over the top of the front cord, moving from left to right, making the first crossing of the cords.

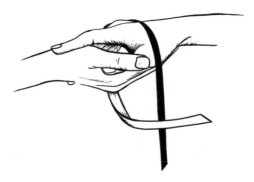

Figure 19: Infinity knot steps 4, 5, and 6

7. The officiant brings the cord in their left hand under the cord in their right, moving from right to left, looping the cord in the back around the front.

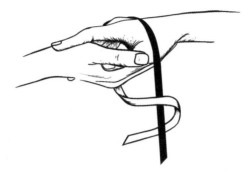

Figure 20: Infinity knot step 7

8. The officiant takes the cord in the back and brings it up to the top of the hands, tucking it under the cords on top of the hands. Now, they tuck it under on the left, pulling it up on the right.

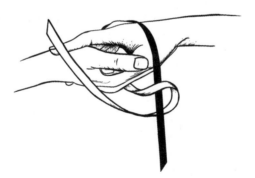

Figure 21: Infinity knot step 8a

Lift the cord so that it is again above the hands...

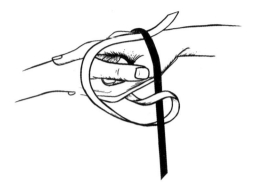

Figure 22: Infinity knot step 8b

… then, from left to right, bring it back underneath.

9. Drape the cord in the back over the back of the hands.

10. The officiant releases both ends of the cords. The knot has been set up. Now we wait for the moment in which the officiant offers a final blessing (or those being joined do in unison), at which time the officiant again grabs both ends of the cords as those being joined slowly and carefully pull away their hands. The officiant then pulls both ends tight, tying the knot.

Figure 23: Infinity knot complete

Ritual Preparation

The officiant should ritually prepare the area with whatever methods their practice or tradition dictates, such as cleansing with smoke or sacred waters, and arranging the items on the altar.

Those being joined should ground and center themselves.

THE RITUAL

Once everyone involved has gathered, we will begin the ritual itself.

WELCOME AND BLESS THE SPACE

The officiant lights the white pillar candle and rings the bell three times to gather the focus of those in attendance. After a moment of silence, they speak aloud a prayer, such as:

> **Beneath the stars, the moon, and sun,**
> **We gather here to witness love.**
> **A joining of [number of partners] hearts as one.**
> **By earth below and sky above.**

The officiant now establishes ritual space by doing the following:
Light the incense and waft the smoke around the altar or stage area. Say:

> **Spirits of air!**
> **Clear our minds and our intentions.**

Light the red candle and move it around the area in front of the altar. Say:

> **Spirits of fire!**
> **Bright our passions and our will.**

Sprinkle the water from the bowl around the general area. Say:

> **Spirits of water!**
> **Soften our hearts and dispel dissension.**

Sprinkle the soil around the general area, or reverently move the stone around the ritual space. Say:

> **Spirits of earth!**
> **Our bodies strong, our focus still.**

A moment of silence is observed, and then the officiant offers a prayer:

> By east and south and west and north,
> By sky above and earth below
> This space is now between the worlds,
> The world unseen …
> And the world we know.
> Between the worlds we speak this truth:
> Love rules eternal.

WELCOME IN SPIRITS

The officiant calls in any divine beings or spirits being invoked, calling upon them to bestow their blessings on the union. Alternatively, the specific partner who works with that spirit can invoke them.

DECLARE THE INTENT OF THE RITUAL

The officiant should speak some inspired words about love and marriage, as well as of those who are being joined, after which those being joined will step up to join the officiant in the area in front of the altar, blessed by the elements.

CLEANSING

Those being joined will now face the altar while the officiant performs a symbolic cleansing on each of them using sacred smoke, bells, salt water, or another method of their choosing. As a symbol of them leaving their old lives and identities behind, they will each offer up an old belonging to be ritually burned or buried. Each should be called upon to state what the belonging is and how it represents their old life. It can then be placed into either the firepit or on the black cloth on the ground, which will then be used to wrap the gathered items together.

Those being joined will now each take an unlit taper candle (with its holder and bobeche) and—holding it in their right hand—light it from the white pillar. Holding their now-lit taper, they will then turn to face each other over or around the cauldron or firepit.

The Vows

Next come the vows. Those being joined should speak aloud their prearranged vows. Once they have all finished speaking, they will simultaneously use their candles to light the fire in the pit or cauldron and together say: "These [number of partners] hearts now shine as one."

As the fire lights, they back away to contemplate how their individual flames have now merged as one and extinguish their taper, handing each to the officiant, who will then place them upon the altar. Alternatively, they may carefully place the lit taper, holder and all, into the empty cauldron while speaking the above.

The Handfasting

Now the officiant rings the bell three times. The partners all face each other in a circle before the altar, allowing for room for the officiant to reach in at the appointed time. They each extend their left hand into the center, joining them together.

The officiant then drapes the cords over their joined hands. Alternatively, you may wish to have individual friends come up to drape a single cord while saying a few words about the person in question or offering a blessing or wish.

After all the cords have been draped over their clasped hands, the officiant will then begin to tie the knot.

The infinity charm is to be said while tying the infinity knot:

> The Muses spin and weave the fates
> Each cord a life and loving heart
> And here now joined as loving mates
> The knot is tied; their new life starts.

They will then signal those being joined to gently release their grip and slowly pull their hands free as the officiant pulls the cords to tighten the knot, often with a charm or blessing as they do so, such as:

> Hand to hand and heart to heart
> A blessing here we do impart.
> May your lives be long with health and mirth
> Blessed by the stars and by the earth.

Those being joined are then pronounced handfasted by the officiant in whatever terminology has been previously agreed upon.

**I now pronounce you [married/handfasted, etc.]
Let us now celebrate your love and your new lives together!**

The Toasting

The officiant rings the bell once and then fills the married partners' chalices with the ritual beverage, offering a toast in their honor with some heartfelt words: "May you always enjoy health and happiness!" for example.

The just-married now kiss or embrace and then leave the area to join the rest of those assembled, or to retreat into another area for whatever additional festivities have been planned.

Close the Ritual

The officiant then acknowledges and thanks any deities or spirits present and thanks the attendees before ringing the bell three times to close the ceremony.

Suggestions and Alternatives

Those being joined can begin masked but then reveal their faces for the vows. (Oh, the drama!)

Those in attendance can be asked to write short blessings or wishes for the partners to be read during the toasting.

The officiant can light the taper of the first to be joined, and then that person will light the taper of the person on their left, and so on, until all tapers have been lit and a "circle of light" has been cast. Then they can all light the white pillar together in unison.

Those being joined can be "crowned" as monarchs for the ceremony. Each monarch can be representative of some different magical, mythological, or natural force that is significant to the individual and the group, such as the three phases of the moon, the four (or five) elements, suits of the tarot, layers of music, animal spirits, plant spirits, etc. What personal energies do those being joined wish to incorporate into their special day? What blessings would they like bestowed upon their life bond?

Coming Out Celebration Ritual

Probably the best-known queer rite of passage is coming out: telling the folks in your life that you're queer. Though you may need to come out repeatedly throughout your life as you connect with new people, when you first reach a point where you're comfortable telling the most important people in your life that you are some flavor(s) of LGBTQIAP2S+, you deserve a party! This ritual is intended to be part of that party, to joyfully acknowledge with your favorite people that you are here, you are queer, and you are proud. This ritual is intended for a group, and adaptations for doing the ritual with a group online can be found after the ritual.

You may be tempted to offer this ritual as a surprise for the person who came out: don't. Coming out is an emotional experience, and the person may not be fully transparent with you about all the ways they're feeling about it, and may not be ready to celebrate it with a group yet. Remember, do not ever "out" someone else or pressure somebody into coming out. It is a deeply personal choice and one that's influenced by personal safety factors, among other things.

I have used the pronouns "they/them/theirs" to refer to the honoree in this ritual, but please swap them out for the honoree's correct pronouns. I've put those pronouns in brackets as a reminder to replace them if needed.

Partners and Energies

The following partners and energies are particularly well-suited for this ritual's task. The power in this ritual comes from the person who came out and their community supporting them.

Partners

If the person being celebrated has specific spirits or deities they would like to include, by all means do so.

ANCESTORS

A call to queer ancestors is included in this rite. You may call whichever queer ancestors you wish, whether they are the stream of power of all the queer people who have existed before us or specific queer people from history.

ENERGIES

+ **Planet:** Sun (for joy and celebration)
+ **Qabala:** Tiphareth
+ **Element:** Water (for community and connection)
+ **Tarot:** Four of Wands, Ten of Cups

RECOMMENDED TIMING

Performing this ritual on any of the following days or at any of the following times will add power to this working.

+ **Day of the week:** Sunday (for Sun)
+ **Planetary hour:** Sun
+ **Moon phase:** Full

RITUAL MATERIALS

+ Either body-safe tattoo markers and a towel, or regular markers and poster board
+ Party decorations—rainbows and colors specific to the person's appropriate pride flag(s).
+ Party food and drinks
+ A chair, decorated to look extra-special
+ Small dish of salt water
+ Incense and a lighter
+ A 30-plus-minute happy Pride music playlist and a device with speakers to play it on

Note: This ritual involves writing on the honoree's body. Before any plans begin, talk to the honoree to assess whether they are comfortable with people writing or draw-

ing on their skin with body-safe markers. If they are not, create a poster representing their body instead.

Additionally, if you are unsure of what colors to use for your décor, you can find which colors to use for various queer identities by searching "[identity] pride flag" online. For example, the transgender pride flag colors are light pink, light blue, and white.

Remember when bringing music into ritual to download the music beforehand. Put your phone on airplane mode or close out any noisy programs on your computer so you aren't distracted by notifications during the ritual.

SENSORY AND EMOTIONAL ENERGIES TO TIE IN

This ritual is a celebration and affirmation. It should be a happy and joyful ritual, kind of like a mini Pride festival.

RITUAL PREPARATION

If using poster board and markers, draw the outline of a person's body on it in black marker, big enough to fill the posterboard so people can write and draw on the body. You can decorate the body a bit with glitter or enhancements, or draw on details to match the person being celebrated, like hair, tattoos, and jewelry. Just make sure you leave enough room for people to add their designs and words to the body.

Tidy up and then cleanse your working space with sacred smoke, a besom, or whatever space-clearing practice resonates with you and your group.

Decorate the space for a party. Set out food and drinks. Put the chair in the center of the circle.

Set the salt water and incense near the entrance of the ritual space. Just before people go into ritual, light the incense.

Set a phone or other music-playing device inside the ritual space, along with the towel and the body-safe tattoo markers or poster board and markers.

Someone should lead the group in a grounding and centering meditation.

As people move into the ritual space, have them dip their fingers in the salt water and dot their foreheads with it, and waft the incense over themselves.

The Ritual

You will now create your ritual container. Have all participants stand in a circle, and hold hands if it's comfortable to do so. Beginning with the person standing in the east, hum a single, low note. After a second or two, the person to their left joins them in humming a single note, either the same one or one that harmonizes, if they have that ability. After a second or two, the person on their left continues, and so on, until the whole circle is humming all at once. Visualize a bubble of protective energy surrounding the space and filling the room. When you feel the circle is cast, stop humming.

Declare the Intent of the Ritual

Have someone say the following: "Today we gather to celebrate [name] coming out. We are so proud of [name], and in this ritual we affirm [their] identity and bless [name] with the love of [their] community."

Welcome in Spirits

If the person being celebrated wishes to call in particular spirits or deities, have them do so now.

You may wish to call to the queer ancestors as well. Say: "We call the queer ancestors, the mighty dead who have taken these paths before us. We ask you to join us in our celebration of [name], to commemorate the brave step [name] has taken by coming out to those [they] hold dear. Lend [name] strength, protection, and wisdom in this ritual, and in the days, weeks, and months ahead. Hail and welcome."

Raise Energy

Someone should say: "To begin, let us celebrate [name] in dance! Let us be joyful and revel in the blessing of [name]!"

Begin playing the playlist, and have everyone dance around within the circle for a few minutes (or as long as you like!). Have fun!

Focus, Direct, and Release Energy

When you're ready, ask the person being celebrated to sit in the chair in the middle of the circle and, if using, set the poster board in the middle of the circle as well. If you're going to be writing on the person's skin, let them dry off a bit with the towel first in case they got sweaty while dancing.

Everyone other than the honoree should continue dancing. One by one, each person should stop dancing and approach the honoree and offer to write or draw something empowering or affirming on them or the poster board representing them. They should first check if the person is okay with the specific thing they want to draw/write and where they are going to draw/write it, even if drawing on the poster board. The honoree needs affirmation, but also bodily autonomy and sovereignty. As each thing is drawn or written on, the person being celebrated should visualize that image or writing sinking into themselves and integrating with their energy. After drawing or writing, each person may offer a verbal blessing to the honoree, then return to dancing.

Give Thanks

When everyone has written on the honoree or poster board, gather once more in a circle.

The honoree may take a moment to thank those gathered and any spirits or deities they invited into the ritual.

If you called in the queer ancestors, bid them farewell. Say: "Queer ancestors, the mighty dead who have taken these paths before us, we thank you for your joyful presence in our ritual this day. We bid you hail and farewell."

Close the Ritual

Everyone should take a deep breath together and visualize the circle created at the beginning melting into the floor. When you feel the energy has fully returned to the earth, someone should say: "This rite has concluded."

And then everybody can cheer!

Post Ritual

Everyone should be sure to have something to eat fairly soon after the ritual to help them ground. And then ... keep partying!

The honoree may want to take a few minutes to journal, draw, or record themselves speaking about their experience while it's fresh in their mind. If you used poster board, they may wish to hang it near their altar, or keep it someplace safe as a reminder of the love and support of their community.

ADAPTATIONS FOR DOING THIS RITUAL WITH A GROUP ONLINE

If you want to do this ritual over video chat, here is how you can adapt it.

Each person should use a purification method of their choice prior to ritual.

Keep the casting the same, but agree ahead of time to an order in which people will join in the sound. Everyone will unmute for this. One person will begin toning, then the next person will join in, and so on. Tell everyone before casting to visualize a circle encompassing everyone on the call.

People can suggest to the honoree what and where to draw on themself, if they are comfortable with that. Alternatively, you can create an online whiteboard, draw the figure there, and have people draw, write, or type on it. The honoree can print it out afterward and keep it.

GENDER AFFIRMATION CELEBRATION FOR TRANSGENDER AND NONBINARY PEOPLE

Sometimes, as trans and nonbinary people, we don't feel like we are welcome or belong within communities of people who share our gender. Impostor syndrome hits hard, and sometimes the people of our gender, in particular cisgender people, simply aren't welcoming or affirming when we come out. Trans women feel excluded from groups of women. Trans men feel excluded from groups of men. And nonbinary people struggle to find and connect with groups of nonbinary people and feel excluded from both trans and cis communities altogether.

Wouldn't it be great if, when someone comes out as their authentic gender, they were welcomed and affirmed by a group of people of that same gender? That's what this ritual is all about. It is intended for a group consisting entirely of people of the same gender identity. For binary trans folks, ideally both cisgender and trans people of the same gender would be included in the ritual, as affirmation by cisgender people can be particularly powerful. For nonbinary folks, only other nonbinary folks should be included.

This ritual leaves a lot of open space for customization based on the gender and desires of the person being celebrated. I encourage you, as with all rituals in this book, to make it unique and specific for the person being celebrated.

After the ritual, you should have a gender-affirming, fun activity planned for all present to enjoy together.

Since a lot of us meet our people in online spaces, there's also a note at the end for how to adapt this ritual to be done online.

Note: I have used the pronouns "they/them/theirs" to refer to the honoree in this ritual, but please swap them out for the honoree's correct pronouns. I've put those pronouns in brackets as a reminder to replace them if needed.

Partners and Energies

The following partners and energies are particularly well-suited for this ritual's task.

Partners

As befits the gender of the person being honored:

+ The Divine Masculine
+ The Divine Feminine
+ The Divine Androgyne

The honoree may choose to also invite deities or helper spirits of their choice.

Energies

+ **Planet:** Sun (for joy and community)
+ **Qabala:** Tiphareth
+ **Element:** Water (for emotions, community, and connection)
+ **Tarot:** Three of Cups

Recommended Timing

Performing this ritual on any of the following days or at any of the following times will add power to this working.

+ **Day of the week:** Sunday (for Sun)
+ **Planetary hour:** Sun
+ **Moon phase:** Full

Ritual Materials

+ A chair for the guest of honor, possibly decorated to look extra-special
+ A small dish of salt water
+ Incense and an incense holder
+ A lighter or matches for the incense, and charcoal if using loose incense

- A special piece of jewelry or accessory for the guest of honor, appropriate for their authentic gender
- Attendees should bring gender-affirming gifts for the guest of honor
- *Optional:* gender-affirming party decorations; a drum, rattle, or other percussion instrument

Note: Consult the honoree ahead of time for what decorations, incense, jewelry or accessory, and kinds of gifts they would find gender-affirming.

SENSORY AND EMOTIONAL ENERGIES TO TIE IN

This ritual is all about celebration and affirmation. The goal is for the person who has recently come out as their authentic gender to feel welcomed, affirmed, and joyful in the presence of other people of that same gender.

RITUAL PREPARATION

Tidy up, decorate (optional), and then cleanse your working space with sacred smoke, a besom, or whatever space-clearing practice resonates with you and those gathered. Set up your altar with the ritual materials. Place the chair in the center of the ritual space. Set up a table for gifts.

Put the salt water and incense near the entrance of the ritual space. Just before people go into ritual, light the incense.

Someone should lead the group in a grounding and centering meditation.

As people move into the ritual space, have them dip their fingers in the salt water and dot their foreheads with it and waft the incense over themselves.

THE RITUAL

You will now create your ritual container. Have all participants stand in a circle, and hold hands if it's comfortable to do so. Beginning with the person in the east, hum a single, low note. After a second or two, the person to their left joins them in humming a single note, either the same one or one that harmonizes, if they have that ability. After a second or two, the person on their left continues, and so on, until the whole circle is humming all at once. Visualize a bubble of protective energy surrounding the space and filling the room. When you feel the circle is cast, stop humming.

DECLARE THE INTENT OF THE RITUAL

Have one person (not the person being celebrated) say the following: "Today we welcome [name] into the fold as a [man/woman/nonbinary person]. Having discovered [their] authentic gender, we affirm and commit to supporting our new [brother/sister/sibling] as [they] begin their journey of [manhood/womanhood/nonbinaryhood]."

WELCOME IN SPIRITS

Have one person (not the person being celebrated) say the following: "We call in the power of the Divine [Masculine/Feminine/Androgyne] to join our rite this day. Bless and affirm [name] with your power as we celebrate [them] as one of our own. We bid you hail and welcome."

If the person being honored wishes to do so, they may welcome in their own deities, allies, and helper spirits in their own words.

RAISE ENERGY

Have the honoree sit in the chair in the middle of the circle.

The rest of the group chants for the guest of honor three times:

With all the magic we hold within
We welcome you, [sister/brother/sibling]
For you are one of us
We affirm you as a [woman/man/nonbinary person]
For you are one of us
You are one of us
You are one of us

If you have a drum, rattle, or other percussion instrument, play it while the group chants.

When you finish chanting, cheer!

BLESSING OF THE JEWELRY OR ACCESSORY

Everyone gathered should hold their dominant hand over the piece of jewelry or accessory. Each person, including the honoree, should take a turn offering a blessing of what they wish for the honoree on their journey as a person of their gender. When everyone has said their blessing, one person should put the jewelry or accessory on the honoree, saying something like: "Welcome, [brother/sister/ sibling]. We love you and wish only the best for you. You are one of us."

THANKS AND FAREWELL

Have one person (not the person being celebrated) say the following: "We thank the power of the Divine [Masculine/Feminine/Androgyne] for joining our rite this day. Please continue to bless and affirm [name] as one of our own. We bid you hail and farewell."

If the honoree called in any divine beings or helper spirits to the ritual, they can bid them farewell in their own words.

CLOSE THE RITUAL

Everyone should return to the place in the circle where they started the ritual and take a deep breath together. As they exhale, they should visualize the circle they cast sinking into the ground. When the circle has fully sunk into the earth, someone should say: "This rite is concluded."

And then everybody can cheer!

POST RITUAL

Give the honoree a few minutes between the ritual and the party to journal, draw, or record themself speaking about their experience while it's fresh in their mind. That's a perfect time for the rest of you to reset the space, have a snack, order takeout, or prepare to head to your next activity.

You should immediately follow this ritual with a gender-affirming party, gift opening, and activity for the honoree. Some ideas: A slumber party, a spa day, axe throwing, racecar driving, clothes swapping or shopping, barbecuing, playing a sport, watching movies about people of the same gender...let your imagination go wild!

ADAPTATION TO DO THIS RITUAL ONLINE

If you'd like to do this ritual online over video, here are some ways you can adapt it. Purchase the gender-affirming jewelry item or accessory ahead of time and send it to the honoree.

Everyone should send the honoree wrapped gifts ahead of time so they can open them after the ritual on camera.

Each person should use a purification method of their choice prior to ritual.

Keep the casting the same, but agree ahead of time to an order in which people will join in the sound. Everyone will unmute for this. One person will begin toning, then the next person will join in, and so on. Tell everyone before casting to visualize a circle encompassing everyone on the call.

For the chant, I would normally recommend having one person keep their mic on while everyone chants so it doesn't sound so dissonant and confusing, but in this case, I recommend everyone have their mics on, because it's so important for the honoree to hear everyone saying those words. You may choose to have each person on the call say the chant and then pass it to the next person to repeat it, rather than everyone saying it at once.

To bless the jewelry or accessory, have the honoree hold it up to their webcam and have each person say their blessing and send energy to it.

The fun activity should be something you can do online. You can watch a movie together, play an online video game, do slumber party/spa things together, etc. Just make it something gender-affirming.

Conclusion

All humans quest for meaning in our lives. If you're reading this book, you're probably particularly conscious of that quest for yourself. Creating rituals around rites of passage and explorations of your inner self can add layers of meaning and depth to your life. They help you to pause and appreciate these anchors of the self and help them resonate more deeply within.

I hope, in reading this book, you've been inspired to think about your rites of passage and gender and sexuality explorations differently, and are considering new and interesting ways to mark those moments with honor and pride as part of your magickal practice.

I hope you have tried or plan to try one of the rituals in this book, and I hope you make it truly your own, customizing it in ways that make sense for you.

As queer people, we have both the challenge and the opportunity to write our own scripts, to determine what is meaningful and worth celebrating. Make your script a good one, and don't be afraid to improvise.

May you and your path be blessed.

Acknowledgments

Huge thanks to Storm Faerywolf, Misha Magdalene, Rev. Ron Padrón, and Brandon Weston, who contributed rituals to this book. Your perspectives and brilliant ideas made this book awesome.

Special thanks to those who graciously contributed their time for research interviews, suggested deities for rituals, offered queer support organizations for inclusion, and offered feedback on the book in process:

- Ivo Dominguez Jr.
- Irene and Ash Glasse
- Alice Juliette
- Phoenix LeFae
- Misha Magdalene
- J. R. Mascaro
- Natasha Nacre
- Rev. Ron Padrón
- Brandon Weston
- Cat Yimet

Thank you to my wonderful life partner, Niall, for his encouragement and support throughout this process.

Thank you to my editor, Heather Greene, for her keen insights and all the helpful feedback that helped make this book better. Thank you to Hanna Grimson, my copy editor, for her thorough work polishing the language and helping this book really sing!

Huge thanks to Shira Atakpu for the gorgeous cover design.

Thank you to my publicist, Markus Ironwood, for all his encouragement and for telling the world about my books.

And thanks to Borislav Slavov, composer of the phenomenal *Baldur's Gate 3* soundtrack, which was the primary musical backdrop for writing this book.

GLOSSARY OF TERMS

Please note that terminology for queer identities is rapidly evolving, so this list is merely an introductory guideline based on when this book was written. New terms and new understandings of these terms may have been determined since its publication.

For more in-depth definitions, I recommend *The A–Z of Gender and Sexuality: From Ace to Ze* by Morgan Lev Edward Holleb.

Agender: A gender identity where someone does not identify with any particular gender and does not feel like any particular gender.

Aromantic (Aro): A sexual identity where someone does not experience romantic attraction or desire for romantic relationships. Much like asexuality, this can be a spectrum.

Asexual (Ace): A sexual identity where someone does not experience sexual attraction. Asexuality is a spectrum and encompasses many different relationships with sex, from being repulsed by it to enjoying it but still not experiencing sexual attraction.

Bigender: A gender identity where someone experiences exactly two gender identities.

Bisexual (Bi): A sexual identity where someone is attracted to both their own gender and another gender or other genders, not limited to just those who identify as men or women. Shares heavy overlap with the term *pansexual*, and the differences between them are nuanced and varied depending on who you ask.

Butch: A queer gender expression, a counterpoint to *femme*, where someone presents in a masculine manner. Historically used in the lesbian community, but its meaning is broadening to include other gender and sexual identities.

Cisgender: A gender identity where someone unambiguously identifies with their gender assigned at birth. Someone assigned female at birth who unambiguously identifies as a woman is cisgender. Likewise, someone assigned male at birth who unambiguously identifies as a man is cisgender.

Cisnormativity: The societal bias that being cisgender is the norm, and assumes cisgender people all express their gender in codified gender roles.

Demiboy or **demimasculine:** A gender identity where someone identifies somewhat, but not entirely, as a boy or man.

Demigirl or **demifeminine:** A gender identity where someone identifies somewhat, but not entirely, as a girl or woman.

Demisexual: A sexual identity on the asexuality spectrum where someone only feels sexual attraction to another person after bonding with them emotionally first.

Feminine-presenting: A gender expression where one exudes qualities typically ascribed to women, including clothing, jewelry, grooming, and behaviors. Not necessarily someone who identifies as a woman.

Femme: A queer gender expression, a counterpoint to *butch*, where someone presents as traditionally feminine. Historically used in the lesbian community, but its meaning is broadening to include other gender and sexual identities.

Gay: A sexual identity where someone is exclusively attracted to people of their same gender. This is sometimes used as a catchall term synonymous with *queer*.

Gender: A set of cultural norms and social roles. Not the same thing as *sex*.

Gender expression: How someone presents their gender to the world. This includes choices of clothing, behaviors, makeup, vocal mannerisms, and more. A person's gender expression may differ from their gender identity.

Genderfluid: A gender identity in which someone experiences at least two fluctuating gender identities, and may also sometimes feel like multiple genders simultaneously or no gender at all.

Gender identity: A person's innate sense and experience of their gender. It may differ from a person's gender expression.

Genderqueer: An identity in which someone experiences their gender in a non-cisnormative way. This is often used as an umbrella term that includes agender, bigender, genderfluid, nonbinary, transgender, and more identities, but can be a personal identifier as well.

Heterocisnormativity: The societal bias that being cisgender and heterosexual are the norm, and assumes all heterosexual cisgender people express their genders and sexuality in similar ways.

Heteronormativity: The societal bias that being heterosexual is the norm, and assumes heterosexual people all express their sexuality in similar ways, e.g., with codified gender roles and not kinky or polyamorous.

Heterosexual: A sexual identity where someone is exclusively attracted to the people who are the binary gender different from their own.

Intersex: A biological identity where someone's sex characteristics do not all neatly fit into either male or female classification.

Lesbian: A sexual identity for women and femmes, either transgender or cisgender, who are sexually and/or romantically attracted exclusively to women and femmes.

LGBTQIAP2S+: An umbrella community label meaning lesbian, gay, bisexual, transgender, queer, intersex, asexual/aromantic/agender, pansexual, Two-Spirit, and more.

Masc or **masculine-presenting:** A gender expression where one exudes qualities typically ascribed to men, including clothing, grooming, and behaviors. Not necessarily someone who identifies as a man.

Nonbinary (Enby): A gender identity where someone does not identify with a binary gender of *man* or *woman*. This is often used as an umbrella term that includes agender, bigender, genderfluid, genderqueer, and more identities, but can be a personal identifier as well.

Pansexual (Pan): A sexual identity where someone is attracted to multiple or all genders, not just men and women. Shares heavy overlap with the term *bisexual*, and the differences between them are nuanced and varied depending on who you ask.

Polyamory: A romantic identity where someone has, or has a consistent desire to have, multiple romantic partners at once, as opposed to monogamy, where someone commits to one romantic relationship at a time. Polyamory is built on the ideas of trust, honesty, and communication among all partners.

Queer: A gender and sexual identity describing people who are not cisgender, not heterosexual, or neither cisgender nor heterosexual. Often used as a catch-all term to describe the LGBTQIAP2S+ community in the most inclusive way possible. Also a verb, *to queer*: to examine that which we consider normal, particularly when related to gender and sexuality; question why that is considered normal and how it came to be considered so; and consider alternatives.

Sex: A set of biological characteristics related to reproductive roles—not the same thing as gender. Also, any act involving genital stimulation and pleasure.

Sexuality: An identity based on who a person is sexually or romantically attracted to or not attracted to, and the types of activities that bring them sexual pleasure.

Sex work: Any work in which sex, in any of its forms, is exchanged for money or resources.

Transgender (Trans): A gender identity where someone does not unambiguously identify with the gender they were assigned at birth. Transgender is also an umbrella term that includes agender, bigender, genderfluid, genderqueer, and nonbinary identities, though people who choose those identity labels may or may not personally identify as transgender.

Two-Spirit: A gender identity held by Native American/Alaska Native people who are not heterosexual and/or are not cisgender. This is a broad umbrella term, and individual Indigenous groups may have other terms in their own languages for queer members of their communities.[21]

---

21. Indian Health Service, "Two-Spirit," accessed December 14, 2023, https://www
.ihs.gov/lgbt/health/twospirit/.

FURTHER READING

The following resources will take your ritual writing, magickal practice, and queer magick to the next level.

RITUALS AND RITES

Learn how to craft powerful rituals for all occasions.

Casting Sacred Space: The Core of All Magickal Work by Ivo Dominguez Jr. San Francisco, CA: Weiser Books, 2012.

Life Ritualized: A Witch's Guide to Honoring Life's Important Moments by Phoenix LeFae and Gwion Raven. Woodbury, MN: Llewellyn Worldwide, 2021.

A Witch's Guide to Creating & Performing Rituals: That Actually Work by Phoenix LeFae. Woodbury, MN: Llewellyn Worldwide, 2023.

QUEER WITCHCRAFT AND MAGICK

Learn more ways to bring your authentic queerness into your magickal practice.

Outside the Charmed Circle: Exploring Gender & Sexuality in Magical Practice by Misha Magdalene. Woodbury, MN: Llewellyn Worldwide, 2020.

Queering Your Craft: Witchcraft from the Margins by Cassandra Snow. Newburyport, MA: Weiser Books, 2020.

Queer Magic: LGBT+ Spirituality and Culture from Around the World by Tomás Prower. Woodbury, MN: Llewellyn Publications, 2018.

Queer Magic: Power Beyond Boundaries, edited by Lee Harrington and Tai Fenix Kulystin. Anchorage, AK: Mystic Productions Press, 2018.

Sacred Gender: Create Trans and Nonbinary Spiritual Connections by Ariana Serpentine. Woodbury, MN: Llewellyn Publications, 2022.

The Satyr's Kiss: Queer Men, Sex Magic & Modern Witchcraft by Storm Faerywolf. Woodbury, MN: Llewellyn Worldwide, 2022.

ASTROLOGY AND PLANETARY TIMING

Make your rituals more powerful by harnessing astrological timing on a deeper level.

Astrology for Real Life: A Workbook for Beginners by Theresa Reed. Newburyport, MA: Weiser Books, 2019.

Practical Astrology for Witches and Pagans: Using the Planets and the Stars for Effective Spellwork, Rituals, and Magickal Work by Ivo Dominguez Jr. San Francisco, CA: Weiser Books, 2016.

Twist Your Fate: Manifest Success with Astrology & Tarot by Theresa Reed. Newburyport, MA: Weiser Books, 2022.

QABALA AND TAROT

Add additional layers of symbolism to your rituals with Qabala and tarot.

Queer Qabala: Nonbinary, Genderfluid, Omnisexual Mysticism & Magick by Enfys J. Book. Woodbury, MN: Llewellyn Publications, 2022.

Queering the Tarot by Cassandra Snow. Newburyport, MA: Weiser Books, 2019.

ANCESTOR VENERATION

Ancestral Whispers: A Guide to Building Ancestral Veneration Practices by Ben Stimpson. Woodbury, MN: Llewellyn Publications, 2023.

QUEER CULTURE AND LIFE

Explore your identity and learn about the history of queerness.

The A–Z of Gender and Sexuality: From Ace to Ze by Morgan Lev Edward Holleb. London: Jessica Kingsley Publishers, 2019.

Gender: A Graphic Guide by Meg-John Barker and Jules Scheele. London: Icon Books, 2019.

How to Understand Your Gender: A Practical Guide for Exploring Who You Are by Alex Iantaffi and Meg-John Barker. London: Jessica Kingsley Publishers, 2018.

How to Understand Your Sexuality: A Practical Guide for Exploring Who You Are by Meg-John Barker and Alex Iantaffi. London: Jessica Kingsley Publishers, 2021.

Queer: A Graphic History by Meg-John Barker and Jules Scheele. London: Icon Books, 2016.

Sexuality: A Graphic Guide by Meg-John Barker and Jules Scheele. London: Icon Books, 2021.

QUEER SUPPORT ORGANIZATIONS

Please note that this is an abbreviated list that is largely biased toward national organizations based in the United States. There are many wonderful organizations doing great work all around the world and in many smaller communities, and I encourage you to research and seek those out.

FOR QUEER PEOPLE IN GENERAL

Consortium (UK)
consortium.lgbt

GLAAD
glaad.org

Human Rights Campaign
hrc.org

Lambda Legal
lambdalegal.org

LGBTQ Freedom Fund
lgbtqfund.org

206 · Queer Support Organizations

National LGBTQ Task Force
thetaskforce.org

PFLAG
pflag.org

Rainbow Railroad
rainbowrailroad.org

SAGE (For Queer Elders)
sageusa.org

SONG (Southern US)
southernersonnewground.org

Stonewall (UK)
stonewall.org.uk

Woodhull Freedom Foundation
woodhullfoundation.org

FOR QUEER PEOPLE OF COLOR

Black AIDS Institute
blackaids.org

National Black Trans Advocacy Coalition
blacktrans.org

Black Trans Travel Fund
blacktranstravelfund.com

Center for Black Equity
centerforblackequity.org

In Our Own Voices
ioov.org

The Marsha P. Johnson Institute
marshap.org

National Black Justice Coalition
nbjc.org

The Okra Project
theokraproject.com

Trans Women of Color Collective
twocc.org

FOR QUEER INDIGENOUS PEOPLE

Navajo Nation Pride
navajonationpride.com

Queer the Land
queertheland.org

Unity Coalition
unitycoalition.org

For Queer Latinx People

Familia TQLM
familiatqlm.org

TransLatin@ Coalition
translatinacoalition.org

Unity Coalition
unitycoalition.org

For Queer South Asian People

Desi LGBTQ+ Helpline for South Asians
deqh.org

Gaysi
gaysifamily.com

NQAPIA
nqapia.org

For Queer Survivors of Abuse

Community United Against Violence
cuav.org

Galop (UK)
galop.org.uk

The Northwest Network
nwnetwork.org

For Queer Children and Teens

Mermaids (UK)
mermaidsuk.org.uk

SMYAL
smyal.org

The Trevor Project
thetrevorproject.org

For Transgender People

National Black Trans Advocacy Coalition
blacktrans.org

Black Trans Travel Fund
blacktranstravelfund.com

Familia TQLM
familiatqlm.org

Forge
forge-forward.org

National Center for Transgender Equality
transequality.org

The Marsha P. Johnson Institute
marshap.org

The Okra Project
theokraproject.com

Trans Justice Funding Project
transjusticefundingproject.org

Transgender Law Center
transgenderlawcenter.org

Trans Lifeline
translifeline.org

Trans Women of Color Collective
twocc.org

FOR QUEER DISABLED PEOPLE

Blind LGBT Pride International
blindlgbtpride.org

ParaPride
parapride.org

Rainbow Alliance of the Deaf
deafrad.org

RespectAbility
respectability.org

Sins Invalid
sinsinvalid.org

For Sex Workers

HIPS
hips.org

Pineapple Support
pineapplesupport.org

Red Umbrella Fund
redumbrellafund.org

SWOP
swopusa.org

Bibliography

Agrippa, Henry Cornelius. *Three Books of Occult Philosophy*. Translated by James Freake. Edited by Donald Tyson. St. Paul, MN: Llewellyn Publications, 1993.

Barker, Meg-John, and Jules Scheele. *Gender: A Graphic Guide*. London: Icon Books, 2019.

———. *Queer: A Graphic History*. London: Icon Books, 2016.

———. *Sexuality: A Graphic Guide*. London: Icon Books, 2021.

Blackthorn, Amy. *Blackthorn's Botanical Magic: The Green Witch's Guide to Essential Oils for Spellcraft, Ritual, and Healing*. Newburyport, MA: Weiser Books, 2018.

———. *Blackthorn's Protection Magic: A Witch's Guide to Mental & Physical Self-Defense*. Newburyport, MA: Weiser Books, 2022.

Book, Enfys J. *Queer Qabala: Nonbinary, Genderfluid, Omnisexual Mysticism & Magick*. Woodbury, MN: Llewellyn Publications, 2022.

Born, Tyler. "Marsha 'Pay It No Mind' Johnson." Out History. Accessed February 23, 2024. https://outhistory.org/exhibits/show/tgi-bios/marsha-p-johnson.

"Can Aquamarine Go in Water?" Moonlight Gems AZ. Accessed February 24, 2024. https://www.moonlightgemsaz.com/can-aquamarine-go-in-water/.

Dominguez, Ivo, Jr. *Casting Sacred Space: The Core of All Magickal Work*. San Francisco, CA: Weiser Books, 2012.

———. *Practical Astrology for Witches and Pagans: Using the Planets and the Stars for Effective Spellwork, Rituals, and Magickal Work.* San Francisco, CA: Weiser Books, 2016.

Dunlap, David W. "Franklin Kameny, Gay Rights Pioneer, Dies at 86." *New York Times.* October 12, 2011. https://www.nytimes.com/2011/10/13/us /franklin-kameny-gay-rights-pioneer-dies-at-86.html

Faerywolf, Storm. *The Satyr's Kiss: Queer Men, Sex Magic & Modern Witchcraft.* Woodbury, MN: Llewellyn Worldwide, 2022.

Giteck, Lenny. "Harvey Milk's Original *Advocate* Obituary from 1979." *Advocate.* November 27, 2018. https://www.advocate.com/politics/2018/11/27 /harvey-milks-original-advocate-obituary-1979.

"Hapi: Egyptian God of the Inundation." *Britannica.* Accessed May 14, 2024. https://www.britannica.com/topic/Hapi.

Harrington, Lee, and Tai Fenix Kulystin, eds. *Queer Magic: Power Beyond Boundaries.* Anchorage, AK: Mystic Productions Press, 2018.

Holleb, Morgan Lev Edward. *The A–Z of Gender and Sexuality: From Ace to Ze.* London: Jessica Kingsley Publishers, 2019.

Iantaffi, Alex, and Meg-John Barker. *How to Understand Your Gender: A Practical Guide for Exploring Who You Are.* London: Jessica Kingsley Publishers, 2018.

Indian Health Service, "Two-Spirit." Accessed December 14, 2023. https:// www.ihs.gov/lgbt/health/twospirit/.

Jones, Cerys R. "Simply the Bes: 7 Reasons Bes Should Be Your Favourite Egyptian God." UCL Researchers in Museums. April 6, 2019. https://blogs.ucl .ac.uk/researchers-in-museums/2019/04/06/simply-the-bes-7-reasons -bes-should-be-your-favourite-egyptian-god/.

Kreider, Tim. "I Know What You Think of Me." *New York Times.* June 15, 2013. https://archive.nytimes.com/opinionator.blogs.nytimes.com/2013 /06/15/i-know-what-you-think-of-me/.

LeFae, Phoenix. *A Witch's Guide to Creating & Performing Rituals That Actually Work.* Woodbury, MN: Llewelyn Worldwide, 2023.

LeFae, Phoenix, and Gwion Raven. *Life Ritualized: A Witch's Guide to Honoring Life's Important Moments.* Woodbury, MN: Llewellyn Worldwide, 2021.

Levey, Jessica. "How to Tie a Handfasting Cord—The Infinity Knot." *American Weddings Blog* (blog). American Marriage Ministries. Updated December 2023. https://theamm.org/articles/595-how-to-tie-a-handfasting-cord -the-infinity-knot.

Magdalene, Misha. *Outside the Charmed Circle: Exploring Gender & Sexuality in Magical Practice.* Woodbury, MN: Llewellyn Publications, 2020.

Penczak, Christopher. *The Temple of High Witchcraft: Ceremonies, Spheres, and the Witches' Qabalah.* Woodbury, MN: Llewellyn Publications, 2017.

Platten, Arhiana. *Rites and Rituals: Harnessing the Power of Sacred Ceremony.* Bethesda, MD: Brave Healer Productions, 2023.

Prower, Tomás. *Queer Magic: LGBT+ Spirituality and Culture from Around the World.* Woodbury, MN: Llewellyn Publications, 2018.

Rea, Sabeau. "LGBTime Machine: Ancient Rome." National Organization for Women. April 5, 2017. https://now.org/blog/lgbtime-machine-ancient -rome/.

Regardie, Israel. *A Garden of Pomegranates: An Outline of the Qabalah.* Los Angeles, CA: New Falcon, 2019.

Rothberg, Emma. "Marsha P. Johnson." National Women's History Museum. Accessed May 14, 2024. https://www.womenshistory.org/education -resources/biographies/marsha-p-johnson.

———. "Sylvia Rivera." National Women's History Museum. Accessed February 23, 2024. https://www.womenshistory.org/education-resources/biographies /sylvia-rivera.

Serpentine, Ariana. *Sacred Gender: Create Trans & Nonbinary Spiritual Connections.* Woodbury, MN: Llewellyn Publications, 2022.

Snow, Cassandra. *Queering Your Craft: Witchcraft from the Margins.* Newburyport, MA: Weiser Books, 2020.

Starling, Mhara. *Welsh Witchcraft: A Guide to the Spirits, Lore, and Magic of Wales.* Woodbury, MN: Llewellyn Publications, 2022.

Uilyc, Ceida. "24 Crystals That You Can and Can't Put in Salt." AllCrystal. Accessed February 24, 2024. https://www.allcrystal.com/articles/list-of -crystals-that-can-go-in-salt/.

———. "How to Cleanse Hematite Crystals," AllCrystal. Accessed February 24, 2024. https://www.allcrystal.com/articles/how-to-cleanse-hematite/.

"Understanding Neopronouns." Human Rights Campaign. Accessed December 22, 2023. https://www.hrc.org/resources/understanding-neopronouns.

CONTRIBUTORS

Storm Faerywolf (he/him) is many things: author, poet, teacher, artist, priest, queer man, warlock. He was drawn to magic as a child, the faeries featuring prominently in his Irish American upbringing, and he dedicated himself to witchcraft in his early teens. He went on to train and be initiated into several streams of traditional and folkloric Craft, most notably the Anderson Faery tradition, where he holds the Black Wand of a Master.

Having taught the Craft for more than thirty years, he is chancellor of Modern Witch University and is a founding teacher of the Black Rose Witchcraft online course. He is a columnist for the Pagan news site *The Wild Hunt* and is the host of the *Witch Power Daily* podcast.

He has written several books, including *The Stars Within the Earth, Betwixt & Between, The Witch's Name*, and *The Satyr's Kiss*. For more, visit faerywolf.com.

Misha Magdalene (she/her), also known as Tamsin Davis-Langley, is a queer transgender witch, priestex, and sorceress with a background in Gardnerian Wicca, Anderson Feri, and grimoiric magic. She is the author of *Outside the Charmed Circle: Exploring Gender and Sexuality in Magical Practice* (Llewellyn, 2020), and has contributed to several anthologies and publications. She has a degree in gender, women, and sexuality studies from the University of Washington. She lives in Providence, Rhode Island with her polymath superhero wife and two adorable black cats.

Rev. Ron Padrón (he/him) is a gay Cuban American hedge priest from the swamps of Florida now living in the mid-Atlantic with his husband and their small cryptid dog. He has been a member of the Pagan community for two decades with specific interests in divination, Queer Ancestor veneration and necromancy, hedge witchery, and spiritual activism. He is the creator of White Rose Witching, through which he manages a blog sharing Queer Ancestor spotlights and rituals and hosts workshops across a variety of topics. He has presented at the Salem Witchcraft and Folklore Festival, Hallowed Homecoming, Free Spirit Gathering, Sacred Space Conference, and local Pagan events.

Brandon Weston (he/him, they/them) is a healer, writer, and folklorist who owns and operates Ozark Healing Traditions, an online collective of articles, lectures, and workshops focusing on the Ozark Mountain region. As a practicing folk healer, his work with clients includes everything from spiritual cleanses to house blessings. He comes from a long line of Ozark hillfolk and is also a folk herbalist, yarb doctor, and power doctor. His books include *Ozark Folk Magic*, *Ozark Mountain Spell Book*, and *Granny Thornapple's Book of Charms*.

© Marcus Dilano Photography

ABOUT THE AUTHOR

Enfys J. Book (they/them) is an author, high priestx, blogger, teacher, performer, singer, songwriter, and comedian. They are the author of the Gold COVR award-winning *Queer Qabala: Nonbinary, Genderfluid, Omnisexual Mysticism & Magick* and coauthor (with Ivo Dominguez Jr.) of *Sagittarius Witch*. They are also a founding member of the "funny, filthy, feminist, fandom folk" band the Misbehavin' Maidens, the creator of a website on queer magick called majorarqueerna .com, and the host of a podcast called *4 Quick Q's: Book Talk with Enfys*, where they interview Pagan authors using questions determined by a roll of the dice. They have taught many classes on magickal rites of passage, tarot, Hermetic Qabala, and queering one's magickal practice at conferences and events around the world. As a nonbinary, bisexual Pagan and performer, Enfys employs a queer lens to break down limiting binaries in magickal practice and advocates for bi, trans, nonbinary/genderqueer, queer, and asexual visibility and inclusion through their writing and music.

TO WRITE TO THE AUTHOR

If you wish to contact the author or would like more information about this book, please write to the author in care of Llewellyn Worldwide Ltd. and we will forward your request. Both the author and the publisher appreciate hearing from you and learning of your enjoyment of this book and how it has helped you. Llewellyn Worldwide Ltd. cannot guarantee that every letter written to the author can be answered, but all will be forwarded. Please write to:

Enfys J. Book
℅ Llewellyn Worldwide
2143 Wooddale Drive
Woodbury, MN 55125-2989
Please enclose a self-addressed stamped envelope for reply,
or $1.00 to cover costs. If outside the U.S.A., enclose
an international postal reply coupon.

Many of Llewellyn's authors have websites with additional information and resources. For more information, please visit our website at http://www.llewellyn.com.